HERE FOREVER

The Timeless Impact of

JOHN SMALE

on Procter & Gamble, General Motors
and the Purpose and Practice of Business

ROB GARVER

ISBN: 978-1-66786-551-5

Printed in the United States of America
First Edition September 2022
Cover art by Frank McElwain

Dedication

To Cathy Caldemeyer, the inspiration and driving force behind this book

and

to the memory of Robert Stanton Garver

Advance Praise for
Here Forever: The Timeless Impact of John Smale
on Procter & Gamble, General Motors and
the Purpose and Practice of Business

"John Smale was that rare leader who was sought out by other leaders, especially when they were facing the toughest of challenges. His ability to see the long view and his deep conviction about doing the right thing for the long term have had a lasting impact on me. This book is a gift of insight for everyone who never had the chance to sit and learn at John's side, as so many of us were honored to do."

Susan Arnold
Board Chair, The Walt Disney Company

"John Smale was one of the great business leaders of his time. This well-written biography tells us what fueled his unparalleled success — specifically, his passion for innovation and his relentless pursuit of excellence."

Ed Artzt
Retired Chairman and CEO, Procter & Gamble

"One of my favorite definitions of leadership is found on a tombstone at Normandy. It reads, 'Leadership is judgment, courage and carelessness of self.' John Smale's life and career add the one missing element: character. This is a book that needs to be read by anyone in a position of leadership. Its examples of people getting it right and people getting it wrong provide priceless lessons for all."

Norm Augustine
Retired Chairman & CEO, Lockheed Martin Corp.

i

"My first reaction, as I began reading this book, was that John Smale led P&G at a time when the world was smaller and simpler. That things have moved on since. That the luxury business I work in now is more complicated and less fact-based.

"But as I kept reading, I started to see things from a different angle. I began to realize that the principles that informed John's leadership are exactly the guiding lights that I rely on, day-in and day-out, to help me navigate the intricacies of my professional responsibilities today — doing the right thing, leadership as a service, managing for the long term, innovation as an engine of growth, focusing on the big picture without losing touch of details and individuals, boiling down thorny issues to fundamental choices, being frank and direct but always fair.

"It is on tough days — when things are complex, when analysis is unclear and decisions are difficult — that I go back to these values. Asking myself what would John Smale do is always a great way to be inspired and cut to the chase!"

Antonio Belloni
Group Managing Director, LVMH Moët Hennessy Louis Vuitton

"Every person should read this book about John Smale. It's a book about leadership, character, values and courage. He was a CEO way ahead of his time!

"I spent the formative years of my 28 years at P&G when Mr. Smale was the CEO. Until I read this book, I didn't realize how much of who I am as a leader today directly flowed from John Smale's DNA as a leader. John always focused on doing the right thing, identifying and growing talent, and making the hard choices that were in the best interest of the Company for the long-term, even if it meant short-term negative consequences. Everyone can learn from John Smale and this fast-paced book."

Chip Bergh
President and CEO of Levi Strauss & Co.

"Very early in his career, John Smale convinced me, just beginning my own career in an advertising agency, that P&G was the company I wanted to work with, not just for a project or two, but for decades. The reason was simple. Though he was just starting his career, he personified P&G's culture — its integrity, its belief in creativity, and its commitment to growing people — in a way that no one I had ever met had done. We did in fact spend decades working alongside one another, building some of the world's greatest brands. He was a remarkable man. I was privileged to know him."

Roy Bostock
Former Chairman and CEO, DMB&B
Former Vice Chairman, Delta Airlines

"If you want to become an impactful leader in the 21st century, read this book. Great leaders honor and learn from the past, meet the challenges of the present in a quality way, and set the table for a more prosperous future. John Smale was a great leader — arguably the best corporate leader of the second half of the 20th century. And, as I understand it, he was an even better human being. The leadership lessons of his storied career are timeless. Learn from him, grow with him, and become the leader you are meant to be."

Douglas R. Conant
Founder, ConantLeadership
Former Chairman, Avon Products
Former President and CEO, Campbell Soup Company

"John Smale graduated from Miami University with a degree in business in 1949. At Miami, we believe that leadership requires vision, integrity, and courage. Throughout his career, John demonstrated all three attributes.

"*Here Forever: The Timeless Impact of John Smale on Procter & Gamble, General Motors and the Purpose and Practice of Business* is an important book for all leaders to read because it reminds us of the need to lead effective organizations that contribute to the communities of which they are part, provide meaning and purpose to those who work for their organization, and constantly innovate (with a long-term view in mind) in order to ensure the organization is sustainable."

Jenny Darroch
Dean of the Farmer School of Business, Miami University

"John Smale's example shows that a leader's sense of time is the hidden source of their power and integrity. Never mind today's buzzwords — we'd all do well to follow Smale's combination of short-term excellence and long-term values."

Zachary First
Executive Director, Drucker Institute

"*Here Forever* captures an essential truth about John Smale: he was totally clear about who he was and what he valued. His commitment to innovation and to excellence never wavered, starting with himself. As a result, he built great brands, renewed great institutions, and helped people grow with confidence, optimism and courage, empowered by his trust. He was a leader we all can continue to learn from, today and forever."

Robert Iger
Retired Chairman and CEO, The Walt Disney Company

"I learned timeless lessons from John Smale: Be principles- and values-led; invest in innovation for sustainable competitive advantage; and focus on growth and value creation for the long term. These leadership lessons have served P&G very well, and they are and will always be relevant to many other companies across a wide range of industries."

A.G. Lafley
Former Chairman and CEO, The Procter & Gamble Company

"John Smale was the leader we all aspire to be. He led The Procter & Gamble Company to codify its Purpose and Values during a seminal time of globalization. He embodied the company's Purpose (improve the lives of the world's consumers) and its Values (integrity, leadership, ownership, passion for winning, and trust). They formed his character. He exemplified this character to the employees of the company. At West Point we work to create leaders of character. That's our mission. Character, Purpose, and Values attracted me to P&G. The desire to be part of something bigger than oneself — something that matters.

"It was my privilege to get to know John better over the last years of his life. The more I got to know him, the more I realized what an authentic leader of character he was. Today, in a world which is increasingly cynical and divisive, being a leader of character matters more than ever. The life of John Smale, captured so well in this book, is an ideal for us all."

Robert A. McDonald
Chairman, West Point Association of Graduates
Retired Chairman, President & CEO of The Procter & Gamble Company
8th Secretary of the Department of Veterans Affairs

"John Smale was one of my closest and dearest friends. He was a man of incredibly strong character and principle and I admired him as much as any man I have ever known. I also had the unique pleasure to experience the 'lighter side' of John when he and his wife Phyllis and my wife Marilyn and I took trips together. He had a great sense of humor. I could write a book about John but that will now not be necessary!"

Charles S. Mechem, Jr.
Retired Chairman and CEO, Taft Broadcasting Company

"True leadership is putting the interest of others ahead of your own , knowing that by doing so you are better off yourself as well. John had plenty of this, and there are many lessons in the way he practiced it.

"John Smale's character was carefully defined by strong values and consistent behavior when it counted most — a lesson all leaders need to understand and, more importantly, practice. I encourage you to read this important book. Impact guaranteed for all who simply want to be better."

Paul Polman
Author, *Net Positive*
Retired CEO, Unilever

"John Smale's life, as explored in this book, is a gift to all who seek examples of extraordinary corporate, community, and family leadership. He is an exemplar of a future-focused visionary whose exceptional skills in business building were only equaled by his uncanny ability to quickly identify and then invest in developing highly effective leaders. The very human side of John's life reminds us that true success always entails having a deep love of and involvement in building strong communities and families. This book provides a rare look into the mind and heart of a very private, humble yet incredible person. It leaves us with inspiration that is applicable to all aspects of our lives."

Janet B. Reid, Ph.D.
CEO, BRBS World, LLC
Member of the P&G Diversity and Inclusion Advisory Board

CONTENTS

Ahead of His Time

John E. Pepper

Former Chairman and CEO, Procter & Gamble

Former Chairman, The Walt Disney Company

John Smale thought in generations, not just in decades and certainly not just in years. He didn't predict the future. He made the decisions necessary to create it.

He was driven by one fundamental conviction about great institutions such as Procter & Gamble and General Motors, two iconic companies that he led through periods of growth, crisis and transformation: They play an essential role in our society, and they are meant to be here forever.

In today's volatile world, that's a conviction worth holding onto. And it's why this book matters to leaders — today and well into the future.

John Smale mastered the art of the long view at a time when many leaders struggled with short-term pressures that often led to short-sighted decisions, which, of course, is truer today than it was even then.

He role-modeled the importance of stewardship, of leaving a company or a brand stronger than it was when you accepted responsibility for it. He believed and invested in game-changing innovation as the only true driver of sustainable long-term growth. And he inspired those around him by placing his trust in them to lead with the clarity and at the same level of excellence that he demanded of himself.

John's standard of leadership shaped the purpose and practice of business as we pursue it today. Decades before most major companies saw and stepped up to their responsibilities to the communities in which they operated and to the planet, John called on business leaders to do the right thing and to do the hard work of earning public trust. He championed diversity and demanded that it be a business priority. He worked to find the right balance between consumer satisfaction, safety and environmental sustainability. He pursued innovation, not just to grow great brands, but to change how business operates to improve people's quality of day-to-day life. And, later in his career as Chairman of the Board of General Motors, he led a major change in corporate governance. He showed what it meant to be accountable not only to shareholders, but also to employees and all the other stakeholders whose lives and livelihoods depend on the enduring success of the institution they are part of.

This book — *Here Forever: The Timeless Impact of John Smale on Procter & Gamble, General Motors and the Purpose and Practice of Business* — brings to life John's enduring impact on the institutions he led and generations of present and future leaders.

It is a journey of discovery. The author, Rob Garver, takes us on that journey, helping us to experience John and his character in the ways that Rob and countless people he talked to saw him.

This book began as a conventional biography, chronicling John's life from his childhood, through his career, and on to his final years. But it ultimately became something more than that. As Rob Garver was discovering the significance of John's life, he experienced a personal loss that changed his own life. That discovery and Rob's loss led to a different book, one full of humanity which brings John's unique qualities to us with striking clarity and inspiration. I believe it succeeds superbly.

John Smale passed away in 2011. Some may ask: "Why write this book now?" For me, the answer is simple. Leaders today are faced with unprecedented and accelerating complexity. I've spent time with many people — some in senior leadership roles, others just beginning their careers, and many others in between — who are trying to respond to the leadership challenges of our time. They're seeking clarity in a world of uncertainty where change is happening at lightning speed. They're looking for examples of exemplary leadership that can guide them.

As you will read, John Smale's life provides an abundance of those examples.

Under John Smale's leadership, Procter & Gamble became a truly global company with the strengthened foundations to stand the test of time. When Smale became President of the company in 1974, P&G's sales were $4.9 billion and its earnings were $316 million. It was operating in 20 countries with a combined population of about one billion people. Twenty-one years later, as he retired from the Board of Directors, sales had grown more than six-fold to $33 billion; profits more than eight-fold to $2.6 billion; and P&G was operating in close to 50 countries with a population of more than five billion people.

These results are an important part of his legacy. But only part.

This book explores a more fundamental question: What makes John Smale's life story so urgently relevant today and timelessly important for future generations of leaders, in business and every other sector of our society?

The answer to this question can be captured in a single, simple word: character. While John Smale demonstrated an abundant mix of leadership strengths — strategic clarity, comfort with risk and a deep belief in the power of people, values and ideas — it was the way he led with character that made him so successful and respected. This is what makes his legacy so timeless.

John's character infused everything he did. It informed his judgment, especially when the way forward was anything but clear. It guided his decisions, particularly the toughest ones. It set the ethical and performance standards to which he held himself and others accountable. And it influenced the way he showed up beyond the boundaries of business — as a husband, father, grandfather, friend and community leader.

I have been privileged to know and work with hundreds of outstanding leaders in my life. Among them all, John Smale stands tallest for me. He brought together wisdom and courage, concern for people, and an ability to balance the short and long term in a manner I've never seen matched. Put simply, he was the most effective executive I've ever known.

————

I worked for John for almost 40 years. I learned from his repeated decisions the importance of doing the right thing for the long term, not the expedient or the comfortable thing. I was inspired by his courage to bet big on the future based not only on the data he saw but even more on the people whose judgment he trusted and character he admired. I watched him treat people with respect and invest personally in their growth and success. I watched him hold people to high standards — the same standards to which he held himself. I saw him focus relentlessly on identifying those individuals who knew what to do to sustain and grow the businesses for which they were accountable.

There was no one to whom I turned more often or with greater confidence during my most challenging days than John. I always knew I would be getting honest wisdom, sharply put.

John's choices and decisions weren't always right. He placed bets that didn't work out. He sometimes waited too long to make what turned out to be the right decision. But he never flinched from facing reality – acknowledging a mistake and acting decisively on the learning from it.

I watched John Smale, over the course of his career, lead with conviction, girded by integrity, principle and his unyielding belief in doing the right thing for the long term.

John Smale titled the collection of his talks published following his retirement with the same words he used to conclude his first address to P&G as CEO: With All That's In Me. What a perfect choice of words. They describe John Smale as I experienced him from the first day I met him until the last day we talked. Those words — "with all that's in me" — described what he brought to every aspect of his life: to P&G, to the community, and to his wonderful family.

The last 15 years of my relationship with John Smale meant the most to me in many ways. I greatly valued his counsel while serving as P&G's CEO and Chairman and our personal friendship deepened. I'll always recall the pride and joy Smale shared as he talked about his children and grandchildren and their progress in school and his fishing trips with them. I'll never forget his love for and closeness with his wife, Phyllis. I can still picture them walking hand-in-hand along the sidewalks near their home. Their relationship remains an inspiration for all of us who knew them.

His example, like the institutions he led and the impact he had, will be here forever.

And I will continue to ask the question that I often asked myself when facing a tough and uncertain decision: "What would John do?"

John Pepper

Prologue

The last time I went fishing with my father was in May 2019, about three months before I started researching this book. It was our annual pilgrimage to Upstate New York to fly-fish for trout on the Ausable River.

It's a part of the world that will always own a piece of my heart. My father was born in Utica, N.Y., a city near the western edge of the Adirondack Park. For years, my family vacationed in the park, and when I think about that place, I am — and will always be — an 8-year-old boy with a hardware-store fishing pole, anticipating the thrill of a fish striking the bait.

After I graduated from college, my father and I, then eventually my brother, my two sisters, and my brother-in-law, began to fish the Ausable regularly, returning to the same stretch of water annually for the best part of 30 years.

For that 2019 trip, my two sons and I flew to Albany from our home outside Washington, D.C., to meet my father and my brother. We had lunch at a diner near the airport, then set off on the 2½-hour drive north to the river.

Dad was a few months shy of his 77th birthday and 18 months removed from successful heart-bypass surgery. He had never been a heavy man, but now he was quite thin. When we reached the river, and Dad began to make his way down the bank toward the water, my brother and I exchanged worried glances.

The name "Ausable" comes from the French "Rivière Au Sable," which translates roughly to "sandy river." French explorer Samuel de Champlain named it after spotting the river's sandy delta from a boat in the middle of the lake that bears his name. But the stretch of river my father stepped into that day was nothing like what de Champlain had seen.

The West Branch of the Ausable is one of the legendary trout streams of the northeastern United States, rising in the High Peaks region of the Adirondack Mountains under the shadow of Mount Marcy. It rushes past the farm where abolitionist John Brown lived, then skirts the town of Lake Placid. For several miles it alternates between wide open flats and dramatic waterfalls before it's finally brought to heel by a dam in the town of Wilmington.

My father's favorite spot is several miles below the dam, but even here, the Ausable can be a difficult river to wade. The current is still strong, and the bottom of the river is strewn with boulders and loose stones. I waited until my sons were in their teens to bring them to the Ausable, largely because I didn't want to spend a whole trip worrying about a skinny 10-year-old losing his footing in deep water.

Now, here I was with the same worries about my father — worries compounded by the fact that Dad was a very aggressive wader.

Long retired by that point, Dad had made a career in New York City as a private banker, projecting an air of sobriety, rectitude and, above all, good judgment. I often wondered how his clients would react to seeing him on a river.

But that first day on the Ausable allayed some of my fears. The river wasn't particularly high, and he was able to wade it with no problem. I convinced myself that things were okay.

———————

This is not the book I set out to write.

Though I hadn't started working on it at the time of that trip to the Ausable, I was already thinking about it. I had been asked to write a business biography, focused on John Smale's years running Procter & Gamble and his time as chairman of General Motors.

I didn't seek out this project. It landed in my lap because I belong to a strange little fraternity of people with one indelible experience in common: We all worked for journalist Bob Woodward on one or more of his best-selling books.

In my case, Woodward hired me in early 2012, and I spent six months all but living on the third floor of his home in Washington, D.C., as we put together what would become *The Price of Politics* in advance of that year's presidential elections.

Bob is one of the most genuinely kind people I have ever met, but he is also absolutely relentless when it comes to getting to the bottom of a story. Working for him — especially under deadline pressure — is an all-consuming experience. People who do it never forget it, and we come away with an understanding that we have passed a sort of test.

A few days before my boys and I got on the plane for Albany, I'd received an email from the writer Bill Murphy, Jr., who had worked for Woodward on two books about the Iraq war.

He had an offer to write a book that he wasn't able to take, Murphy explained. Without mentioning the subject's name, he said it was about the former CEO of a Fortune 50 company.

When we connected on the phone, Bill told me the project was about John Smale, the former head of Procter & Gamble who had retired, only to find himself leading a boardroom coup at General Motors a few years later.

That was intriguing, so I decided to do a little research. I was immediately struck by how little material about Smale was available. There were no existing books about his career, and only a few mentioned him at any significant length. He had evidently been publicity-shy as a corporate executive and even more so in his retirement. The interviews he gave were mostly just-the-facts assessments of P&G's or GM's business at a specific point in time, with little else.

Even the otherwise breathless coverage of the decapitation of General Motors' executive leadership in 1992, in which Smale played a central role, rarely included anything revealing about the man himself.

One thing reliably mentioned in every obituary I could find was that Smale had single-handedly convinced the American Dental Association to endorse P&G's Crest — the first toothpaste to contain fluoride — as an effective means of preventing tooth decay. At the time, it was unheard of for a medical association to endorse a consumer product, and the impact on Crest's sales had been dramatic, vaulting it to market leadership practically overnight.

GM and Crest both made for good stories. Either one, it occurred to me, could have been the subject of a book all by itself.

In fact, I was somewhat surprised that Smale hadn't written one himself. That summer, the business press was full of buzz about an upcoming memoir by former Walt Disney CEO Robert Iger. It seemed to me that, given his résumé, Smale would easily have generated that kind of interest in the 1990s.

I told Bill I was interested, and he copied me on an email to Cathy Caldemeyer, John Pepper and Jim Stengel. Cathy is Smale's daughter, the driving force behind the project. Pepper is himself a former CEO of Procter & Gamble, and Stengel retired as P&G's global marketing officer.

It all seemed straightforward enough, at the time.

In the end, though, there would be nothing straightforward about this book — not for me. I had no way of knowing it, but I was actually embarking on a journey that would force me to come to terms with death, loss and the question of what it means to live a good life.

In addition to passing on a love of fishing, my father also helped me learn to love photography. He had become an accomplished photographer in his retirement, and with his advice and instruction, I eventually became a respectable amateur in my own right.

On the Ausable in 2019, I split my time between the river and the bank, taking pictures when I wasn't fishing. On our last evening there, with the light fading, I was on a steep bank above my father when I saw his left hand snap back above his shoulder and the tip of his rod flex toward the middle of the river.

I raised my camera and, about a minute later, took a picture that I keep in my office today. It's of my father, looking away from the camera in semi-profile. In his left hand, held high, his rod is bent back on itself in an elongated U-shape. His right hand holds the wooden handle of his net as he reaches out to land the last fish I ever saw him catch.

PART ONE

CHAPTER 1

The Foundation of Business

My first real introduction to the personality of John Smale was a love letter. It arrived at my house with a random assortment of news clippings and photocopies a few days after I returned from the Ausable. In a series of conversations with Cathy Caldemeyer and John Pepper, I had expressed cautious interest in learning more about the project. The package, I sensed, was meant to sharpen that interest.

The love letter was on top.

"Dear Pinky," it began. "Pinky" had to be Smale's wife, Phyllis, I assumed. I checked the date — July 20, 1946. I knew enough by then to gather that Smale would have been 18 at the time and in the Navy, where he served a short stint as a seaman first class.

Smale explains that he is typing the letter, rather than writing it by hand, in order to save time. The reason his time is short, he explains, is that senior officers, even admirals, are so frequently asking his opinion on naval matters.

A few lines later, he is a besotted teenager, begging her to send him a picture of herself.

The pile of documents had more materials in it. I picked up a news clipping about a speech Smale gave in St. Louis in 1977, as the Carter administration prepared a wide range of new restrictions on corporate America.

Smale, by then the president of P&G, adamantly opposed more regulation. However, he said much of the blame for new restrictions lay with the business community itself.

The government was stepping in because the public no longer trusted businesses to act responsibly, he said. Public trust of both the government and business was near an all-time low, he added, and President Jimmy Carter had been elected on a very clear promise to restore a sense of "morality" to both.

Smale listed a number of things that made Carter's arguments resonate with voters.

"Is the manager of any business enterprise worth a million-dollar salary? I don't know. One could certainly argue that he is. But how does the public see it?" he asked. "How does the public see the cabin cruiser or the yacht maintained at company expense? The fishing or the hunting lodge? The country club membership or flying the corporate jet to a golf tournament? I'm not suggesting these cannot be legitimate business activities, but what does the average person think?"

Further down in the package, I found the text of a similar speech delivered that year; apparently Smale had given the talk to multiple audiences.

He explained that he wanted business to send a very different message to the public —that corporations were a net benefit to their communities and to the country at large — and he warned of dire consequences if this effort failed.

"The foundation of a strong corporate structure in America must be based on public trust in the integrity and performance of the business community," he said. "All the rhetoric and theory in the world won't do a thing unless business has that trust. And trust is earned by actions — by doing not just what is legal but what is right."

I was intrigued. Smale was making a case for a form of capitalism that recognized more stakeholders in the future of a company than just its shareholders.

He was, I thought, really swimming against the tide. This latter speech was delivered seven years after the economist Milton Friedman published a seminal article in the *New York Times* declaring that the only responsibility of a business was to increase its profits. Friedman argued that any business that "takes seriously its responsibilities for providing employment, eliminating discrimination, avoiding pollution and whatever else may be the catchwords of the contemporary crop of reformers ... [are] preaching pure and unadulterated socialism."

I didn't know much about John Smale at the time, but I was confident he hadn't been a socialist and that nobody attending one of his speeches would mistake him for one.

Friedman's view of the responsibilities of a corporate executive would usher in the era of "shareholder value" as the be-all end-all of corporate governance. It provided the intellectual underpinning for a widespread decline in the belief that business had an obligation to contribute to the general welfare of its employees and its communities.

Yet Smale, the president of a publicly traded company, was making the case in 1977 that a corporation had to display "good citizenship" that extended as far as involvement in community affairs.

"A corporation must regard itself as a true citizen of the community in which it operates, pulling its weight to help solve community problems, because it knows that the health and welfare of the community are important to its own health and welfare," Smale said.

This was the kind of statement that Friedman and his followers dismissed as pious nonsense. But as I went back over the speech, I began to appreciate its complexity.

Smale's starting point had not been to declare that businesses had social responsibilities. Rather, it had been to assert that businesses operate best when they are regulated least — and that the only way to assure a light regulatory burden is for businesses to behave in a way that proves their trustworthiness.

"Today ... good performance in the efficient production of goods is not enough," he said. "Indeed, if corporations are to be free to perform this basic function in the future, they must recognize that the manner and the means employed to achieve the end are as important as the end itself. In essence, in carrying out its function, business must set an example in its conduct that merits public confidence."

In 2019, the Business Roundtable — a lobbying group that represents the CEOs of America's largest companies — issued a new "Statement on the Purpose of a Corporation." It dispensed with the concept of "shareholder primacy," 49 years after Friedman's essay in the *Times*. Instead, it proposed that a company has an obligation to all of its stakeholders — customers, suppliers, employees and community members, as well as its shareholders.

Smale, I reckoned, had them beat by at least 42 years.

A few weeks later, I flew to Cincinnati to meet with Cathy and John. It was late June 2019, on the morning after the second debate of the Democratic presidential primary. I'd been on assignment covering the debate, and I'd filed my story a few minutes before one a.m., giving me about three hours of sleep before I had to get up and catch an early morning flight.

The major airport nearest to Cincinnati is actually across the Ohio River in Kentucky, so when I arrived, I took a cab into the city, spotting the identical towers of the P&G headquarters building from the bridge.

It was a bright sunny day, and I was a little early, so I had the cab driver drop me off some distance away from Pepper's office, thinking I'd walk a while and familiarize myself with the city John Smale had called home.

I realized almost immediately that this was a mistake. The temperature was already north of 80 degrees and rising, and I was in a long-sleeved shirt with a sport coat over it. By the time I made it to the office building, I had shed the jacket, but I was miserably hot, feeling the effects of a night with little sleep, and worried about just how noticeably I had sweated through my shirt.

We were meeting in Pepper's office on the 15th floor of a building across the street from the P&G headquarters campus. The plan for the day was to chat for a short time before walking over to the P&G corporate archive, to look at its collection of materials related to Smale. Then we would have lunch, and I'd conduct separate interviews of Cathy and John.

I was led into a conference room with a panoramic view looking out onto downtown Cincinnati and across the river to Newport and Bellevue, Kentucky. Unfortunately, the sun was streaming into the room, and I was sitting directly in its glare. Already hot and tired, I felt myself begin to sweat even more. I resolved to mention that I'd been up late covering the debate at my first opportunity, just in case I passed out in the middle of the meeting.

I was particularly interested to get a sense of Pepper and what he thought of the project's potential. In addition to being the CEO of P&G, he had also been chairman of the board of the Walt Disney Corp. It was one thing for Cathy to think her father's story merited a book. Pepper, I assumed, would come to the project with a little more detachment.

Sweltering in that conference room, I got my first real sense of the impact that John Smale had had on his colleagues.

Gray-haired, thin, and whip-smart, the 81-year-old Pepper was even more passionate about the idea than Cathy had seemed to be.

"John Smale was the single most inspirational leader I have ever known," Pepper said. He described a man of dedication and vision, who turned Procter & Gamble into a truly global enterprise, doubling the number of countries where the firm operated and laying the groundwork for expansion that would eventually make P&G's non-U.S. sales nearly double its domestic sales.

Smale was also passionate about innovation, Pepper continued. He had no scientific training himself, but he became an evangelist for research and development. He was willing to bet big on new technology and product lines that could give P&G an advantage over its competitors.

This wasn't all news to me. I had done enough background research to understand the arc of John Smale's career at P&G. Still, Pepper's ardor was palpable and compelling.

After a while, Pepper suggested we step outside and walk over to the P&G archives. To my surprise, I realized I was feeling better, and the thought of heading back out into the heat didn't seem like such a big deal.

The P&G headquarters complex takes up two full city blocks, but the buildings themselves fill only about half the area, forming an L-shape along the north and east sides. Most of the remainder is green space, with three large square expanses of grass, each surrounded by a peristyle of cement columns topped by a web of wooden beams that support acres of wisteria vines.

Cathy mentioned, as we crossed the street, that her mother had been influential in the decision to devote so much of the land to open space — something that could be enjoyed by all of Cincinnati.

If John Smale's passion had been P&G, she told me, Phyllis's had been gardening — and not in the sense of a few rosebushes. She had led efforts to beautify neglected areas of Cincinnati; pocket parks and manicured green spaces throughout the city existed largely because of her advocacy.

As with most corporate headquarters in America in the post-9/11 era, getting into P&G's offices is only slightly less difficult than getting on an airplane. After we were granted entry, we headed toward the archive, but our progress was delayed by people who kept recognizing Pepper and stopping to speak with him. Many would not have been born before he retired, yet they knew exactly who he was.

The P&G archive was not the dusty basement room I expected. In fact, it was a professionally curated museum of the company's history. Early packages of Ivory Soap, the company's first blockbuster product, were displayed alongside historic photographs and memorabilia.

A recurring theme in the exhibits is the company's emphasis on innovation, and the archivists preserve small mementos of "Eureka!" moments like the relics of saints. One exhibit contains a wooden mop handle, fitted with a flat block at the bottom. Attached to the bottom of the block are a pair of menstrual pads. Secured to the mop handle is an upside-down bottle of Mr. Clean detergent, with a plastic tube leading from the cap to the pads on the bottom of the block.

It took me a moment to realize that I was looking at a proof-of-concept model for the Swiffer WetJet that was sitting in my kitchen at home.

What also struck me immediately was the prominence of what the company historian, Shane Meeker, had dubbed the "Wall of Failures." The company was dedicating prime exhibit space to products that had bombed. Meeker explained that the purpose was two-fold.

The first was to remind everyone at P&G that a dedication to innovation necessarily entails the acceptance of failure. On the wall is a quote from electric car pioneer Elon Musk: "If you're not failing, you're not innovating enough."

The second purpose was to remind employees to learn from their failures. Each element of the exhibit includes an explanation of what went wrong, in the hope that mistakes won't be repeated.

Meeker rolled out a cart of materials to show me what I'd have to work with if I were hired to write the Smale book. It was a researcher's dream: boxes and boxes of speeches, letters and records documenting Smale's more than 40 years with P&G.

I left with a printout of Smale's own "oral history" of his time at the company, the product of hours of interviews with a previous company archivist.

Walking with Cathy and John to the Queen City Club for lunch, I thought about some other research I had done on John Smale, which I hadn't mentioned to them.

I had gone looking for dirt. I had no doubt that John Smale's family and P&G would be presenting the best possible picture of the man. I wanted to find what they would be tempted to leave out.

I had searched newspaper archives and court records, wanting to make sure I wouldn't get any unpleasant surprises if I committed to the work. I found nothing remarkable, except for one book, by a former *Wall Street Journal* reporter. It was written in the style of an exposé, and by the author's estimation had relied on interviews of hundreds of current and former employees, consultants, competitors and others, as well as examination of thousands of pages of court documents.

The book came out in 1993, which meant that Smale had been P&G's CEO for nine of the 12 years prior to its publication, and its tone was unremittingly hostile to the company. If there was significant dirt on John Smale, I assumed I would find it here.

I bought an electronic copy of the book and ran a quick search. I was surprised to find that, in a 456-page book about a company he ran for nearly a decade, Smale's name appeared just 78 times. I began checking each occurrence.

There were complaints from a former P&G vice president who felt Smale hadn't sufficiently valued his opinion. An employee of a company that P&G bought under Smale's leadership didn't like the way the subsequent merger had been managed. Another person complained that Smale spent too much time trying to decide on what packaging for certain products ought to look like.

The only allegation that looked serious involved the marketing of Rely tampons in the late 1970s and early 1980s. The author claimed that, as president, Smale had suggested going forward with the development of a new version of Rely, even as the company was receiving reports that would later link the tampon to a deadly disease, toxic shock syndrome.

The book presented what seemed like pretty damning evidence. A report from the Centers for Disease Control and Prevention, issued in the spring of 1980, had identified a possible relationship between toxic shock syndrome and menstruation. The author described the CDC report and, in the very next sentence, wrote how "that same spring" Smale had sent the memo to his boss.

That seemed pretty cold-blooded, so I tapped on the link to a footnote, which revealed that the author had a copy of the Smale memo, dated May 14, 1980. I pulled up a newspaper archive and searched for stories about the CDC's initial report on toxic shock syndrome. There were dozens of hits — it would have been practically impossible for Smale to be unaware of the report.

But one thing stood out: the dateline on every story. The CDC had released its report on May 22, eight days *after* Smale had sent the memo.

If this was the worst a motivated reporter could dig up, I thought, the reality of John Smale might actually match the picture that John Pepper and Cathy were painting.

———————

Cathy had secured a private room at the Queen City Club, an institution in downtown Cincinnati since the 1870s. Inside the building, which takes up most of a city block, members can relax in plush armchairs and look up at the wooden paneled walls hung with paintings by famous American artists.

After a pleasant lunch, Cathy left the room, and I began an interview with Pepper. It was an odd situation, interviewing someone who is simultaneously assessing your skills as an interviewer, but Pepper's intense interest in the topic made it go more easily than it might otherwise have.

I asked him to describe a defining moment illustrating Smale's leadership.

Without hesitating, he said, "There are two defining scenes, and they both have the same message."

The first scene he set for me was in Smale's office in 1985. P&G was considering a major acquisition: Richardson-Vicks, a closely held beauty and healthcare products firm, was the target of a hostile takeover by P&G's rival, Unilever. Richardson-Vicks had approached P&G with the suggestion that it step in as a "white knight" and acquire the company itself.

It's hard to overstate the significance of this moment. Unilever was P&G's biggest competitor and had substantial operations in countries where P&G was trying to make inroads. Richardson-Vicks had multiple business units overseas, and securing them would strengthen P&G's competitive position. Losing them to Unilever would put P&G further behind.

Pepper described an early October day when six of P&G's most senior executives surrounded the CEO's desk, bleary-eyed from a week of urgently compiling the due diligence on Richardson-Vicks.

A voice crackled over a speakerphone. It was Geoff Boisi, a Goldman Sachs partner who was advising P&G on the deal.

"I'd recommend to you all that you go up another dollar a share," Boisi said.

Boisi's implication was clear: P&G wasn't the only company interested in being Richardson-Vicks' white knight, and upping the offer was the best way to keep challengers at bay.

P&G was already offering $68 per share for Richardson-Vicks — far above the $60 per share that Unilever had promised investors, and more than $1 billion in total. There was a strong sense among some in the room that P&G was already paying too much. Now Boisi wanted them to tack another $17 or $18 million onto the price tag. The grumbling began immediately, but Smale's voice sliced through it.

"We'll go up the dollar a share," he declared.

P&G won the bidding war and went on to close what, to that point, was its largest acquisition ever.

Pepper immediately launched into a second story.

Again, the setting was Smale's office, about a year before the Richardson-Vicks deal. P&G had struggled for several quarters but was preparing to roll out a series of major new products that, the company was convinced, would get its numbers back on track.

In the meeting, as Pepper recalled, Smale was presented with a choice. P&G would be releasing its annual financial results in a few months, and as things stood, the company would have to report that profits had decreased on a year-over-year basis — the first such decline in decades.

However, executives in the meeting pointed out that Smale had a way to avoid that embarrassment.

The three big products in the pipeline — liquid Tide detergent, an innovative shaped diaper, and a new flavor of Crest toothpaste — would devour millions of dollars in advertising support in advance of their launch. Instead of committing that money immediately, as was its normal practice, the company could simply meter out that support over the coming year. Doing so would allow P&G to show that profits had risen, not fallen, on a year-over-year basis, at the expense of making the rollout of the three new products less effective.

"I'll always remember the decision," Pepper told me. "It's not just the decision he reached, it was how he reached it, which was in a matter of almost a millisecond."

Of course the company would provide full marketing support for the three new products, Smale said. He would tolerate the embarrassing headlines and the temporary hit to P&G's share price, he added, because the company was pinning its hopes for future growth on those three products.

"Those are two stories that epitomize doing the right thing and doing what's right for the long term," Pepper told me.

"I came to know John as a person of enormous integrity," Pepper said. "You'd never have any doubt where you stood. Enormous commitment to the long term. Enormous commitment, while tough-minded, to people."

Eventually, Cathy replaced Pepper in the chair across from me, and we began talking about the father, rather than the CEO.

Up to this point, practically everyone I had asked about Smale had spoken with some degree of reverence about the man. But it didn't take long to realize I'd be getting a more nuanced take from his daughter.

She told me about a man she obviously loved and respected. But she also described a man who, while running the city's largest and most important company, had felt very distant to his children.

"I always wanted more of both my parents' attention," she said.

Cathy said her father could be tough on his children when, for example, he felt they weren't trying hard enough at school. But the toughness was never physical, just disapproving, which stung just as much. Cathy said she could remember being spanked by her father only once — surely an anomaly for a child born in the 1950s.

Her father, Cathy told me, seemed to be able to recognize any façade, to slap aside any lame excuse.

He also had very clear views on money and what it meant to earn it. By the time Cathy was in high school, Smale had moved the family into a big home on a wooded four-acre lot in one of the city's wealthiest enclaves, but he was determined that his children would not grow up with a sense of entitlement.

"He believed in earning money through your own labors," she said.

She remembered standing at the table during high school, asking for a few dollars to go out with her friends and being harangued by her father about the value of money and hard work. Finally Phyllis, in frustration, interrupted with, "Oh, John. Just give it to her."

"He believed in making it on your own," Cathy told me. "And he believed that money did not make you happy. And he also believed that, if you wanted it, you needed to earn it. He had done that for himself and for his family, and he wanted it for his kids, too."

During our conversation, Cathy shared something else — her family's struggle with dyslexia.

All four Smale children had exhibited some degree of the learning disorder, which can have various effects, but generally makes it difficult to read and comprehend the written word.

Dyslexia had seriously affected the academic careers of at least two members of the extended Smale family, and others had almost certainly struggled with undiagnosed cases in the years before the disorder became better understood.

Her father, Cathy added, had almost certainly been dyslexic, as well. He was a terrible speller, she said, and took a long time to read things. However, she added, once he had read something, his ability to recall it was near total.

On the plane home, sitting back in my seat as we gained altitude for the hop over the Appalachians, I thought about the project I was being offered.

Smale was clearly a major figure in U.S. business history, one whose career hadn't been meaningfully explored by anyone. I would have the cooperation of his family and, Cathy and John had assured me, dozens of former colleagues at P&G. Importantly, I'd also have the cooperation of P&G itself.

On the other hand, the book project would mean giving up some freelance relationships that might be difficult to replace if things went south.

I'd need to talk to my wife about it. Beyond the financial implications, I wanted her opinion on the project itself. If this book was going to be of interest to anyone, it was likely an audience of business executives, which she was.

Still, I was already leaning toward making the commitment to Cathy and, by extension, to John Smale.

Back at home, I paged through the oral history document that I'd received at the P&G archives. Nearly 50 pages of single-spaced print, without so much as a line break to mark the change in speakers. It was difficult to read and followed no obvious theme. But what I was after was, unsurprisingly, one of the first things Smale was asked to discuss.

I wanted to see how Smale himself accounted for the seminal event in his career with Procter & Gamble. In 1958, when he was 30 years old, Smale was promoted to associate advertising manager of the company's Toilet Goods division, a move that placed Crest toothpaste in his portfolio.

What happened next was the stuff of legend within the company. Crest had been introduced to the public in 1955, advertised as particularly effective against tooth decay because it contained fluoride. The public was unimpressed, and after three years, the brand hadn't been able to crack 10% in market share.

Not long after Smale took over, the Benton & Bowles advertising agency approached Smale with a new proposal for marketing Crest. Playing up the benefits of fluoride, it would show happy children rushing home from the dentist's office, clutching a report and announcing, "Look, Mom — no cavities!"

Smale instantly recognized its brilliance and happily signed off. The company contracted with artist Norman Rockwell to produce more than a dozen pictures for the print campaign, and the results were almost immediate. Crest's market share hit 10%, and then 13%.

Smale, I knew, had spent the first few years of his stint overseeing Crest in regular dialogue with the American Dental Association. The hope was that the ADA would formally recognize Crest as effective at preventing cavities.

By late 1959, P&G had produced so much research documenting Crest's ability to fight tooth decay that Smale was able to go to the ADA's professional staff and argue that it was irresponsible for the organization to continue ignoring it. The ADA's executive director, Harold Hillenbrand, had come to know and respect Smale, and he agreed that the public health benefits of a broad reduction in tooth decay — particularly among children — ought to outweigh the association's qualms about endorsing a consumer product.

Finally, in August 1960, the ADA announced that its Council on Dental Therapeutics had granted Crest "provisional acceptance." The next day, trading in Procter & Gamble shares was briefly suspended on the New York Stock Exchange because it was impossible to process all the buy orders. When the dust settled, the company's share price had rocketed up 15%.

Little more than a year later, Crest had claimed a 28.1% share of the toothpaste market, passing Colgate and continuing its upward trajectory well into the 1970s.

The Crest story was foundational to Smale's history with P&G, and I was curious to see how he would describe it.

What I expected was a recounting of Smale's own past glories. What I got, instead, was a list of all the other people who had played a role in the brand's success.

More than 40 years after the triumph that made his own name at P&G, Smale remembered the name of the husband-and-wife team at Benton & Bowles who had created the "Look, Mom — no cavities!" campaign, the P&G technologist who had worked with the ADA's scientists to try to earn the group's endorsement, and the University of Indiana scientist who had helped invent the technology behind the fluoride that made Crest work.

The interviewer tried, but he couldn't get Smale to claim personal credit for any part of one of the biggest triumphs of his career.

He took one last shot.

"Can you say, definitively, for the history of Crest, who was the person that said, let's get the ADA to endorse this product?" he asked Smale.

It was a fastball across the middle of the plate. Smale could easily have taken credit and moved on to the next topic, but his answer was clear: "No." The plan had evolved over years, he explained, and much of the essential work on it had been completed before he had any association with the brand.

As I kept working my way through the dense transcript, I was struck again and again by Smale's tendency to dole out credit for P&G's successes, identifying people multiple levels below the C-suite who were instrumental to the company's wins.

Another thing that struck me as I read was the degree to which Smale had changed P&G while CEO. John Pepper had told me about the company's international expansion under Smale and its move into the health and beauty care industries, but I hadn't appreciated how thoroughly Smale had restructured Procter & Gamble from within at the same time.

The oral history explored how, over the course of a few years, Smale had overhauled the company's supply chain management system, scrapped a decades-old divisional structure in favor of a category management structure that eliminated layers of middle management, and instituted a new executive compensation arrangement that tied managers' pay not just to profit but also to broader goals, including diversity.

Setting aside the oral history, I looked up the timing of P&G's performance under Smale. I knew that there had been explosive growth — the multiple acquisitions he engineered virtually guaranteed that. But I also figured that the growth would have been tempered by the internal restructuring — that it would take a few years for the results to shine through.

That wasn't the case. After a small decline in profits in the mid-1980s, P&G under Smale started rising at a remarkable clip, with sales and profits growing at more than 10% per year.

Then, at the end of 1990, with the company in the midst of that epic run, Smale stepped offstage, retiring at the relatively young age of 62. Why the hell would he do that? I figured there had to be a story there.

By the end of June, I was hooked. I sat down and wrote out a proposal for Cathy, and she accepted it. I needed to wrap up some outstanding projects, but in my head, I was already thinking about how I would tell the story of John Smale.

CHAPTER 2

Any Living Company Has Got to Have Growth

I had planned to begin work on the book at the beginning of September, but I hadn't accounted for John Pepper.

The former P&G CEO was as committed to the book as Cathy was, and he had no intention of waiting until September to start bringing me up to speed. Before long, my email inbox was bursting with messages from him, telling me about P&G alumni he had reached out to for the story. His assistant was compiling a spreadsheet for me to use when I needed to contact people.

Pretty soon, Pepper's contacts started reaching out to me themselves, eager to begin sharing stories about Smale. I found it remarkable and more than a little overwhelming.

They sent anecdotes and tributes. I heard from people who were so junior to Smale at P&G that they had at most a handful of interactions with him, yet they had kept and curated the memory of those moments for decades. People who knew him more closely wrote and called, offering their time and assistance.

One former P&G finance executive, David Walker, sat down and wrote a 2,000-word appreciation of Smale. His conclusion knitted together much of what I was hearing from others who had known and worked with him:

Through all of these interactions with John, he was remarkably consistent in his values and behaviors. He was clearly the most professional manager I have ever worked with. Perhaps John raised his voice or swore sometime in his life, but if he did, I never heard it. He was incredibly smart and wise. His focus was on the consumer, the Company, setting the proper tone and culture, and our employees.

I never saw him duck or postpone a tough decision. He was a genuinely good person, along with all of his other talents. He took the time to coach and develop an eager young manager, despite the enormous workload and responsibilities he handled.

I spent the beginning of September laying the groundwork for a reporting trip to Cincinnati. I was planning on several days, split between the P&G archive and interviews with people who had been close to Smale.

But not everyone I needed to talk to was in Ohio; many had retired and moved away. Before I left, I wanted to speak with two, in particular: Gordon Brunner and A.G. Lafley.

Brunner had retired as chief technology officer of P&G and had known and worked with Smale for decades. Lafley had served as CEO of the company, not once but twice, and had come up through the ranks of senior management while Smale ran the company.

I wanted to speak with Brunner about Smale's commitment to innovation at P&G. The company's best financial results were historically driven by products that set themselves apart from competition through superior performance.

It was a major through-line in the history of the company: Tide detergent was the first synthetic soap ever marketed — its predecessors were all derived from animal fats — and it performed so much better than the competition when it was released that it put P&G on top of that segment of the market, where it has remained. The same had been true of Crest, once it received the ADA's seal of approval, and later, Pampers disposable diapers and Bounty paper towels.

The public profile of Procter & Gamble was a company dedicated to saturation advertising of its products. But marketing genius gets you only so far if your product is inferior to the competition.

Smale knew that, Brunner told me. But more importantly, he said it out loud. He had become CEO during an uncharacteristically dry spell for P&G with new products.

Brunner recalled an interview Smale gave to P&G's in-house magazine, *Moonbeams*, shortly after becoming CEO. In the piece, Smale said, "Products like Pampers, Crest and Tide don't come along very often, but they show our enormous commitment to research. We can market our products on a par with anybody, but the real difference at this company is product innovation and research."

To outsiders, the weight of that statement wouldn't have been obvious. But within the company, Brunner said, it was clear that Smale was putting down a marker.

P&G had pioneered the very concept of "brand management." It was the biggest advertiser in the world. If you asked anyone where the company's center of gravity lay, they'd have told you it was within its marketing operation.

By declaring that research and development was at the heart of the company's success, Smale simultaneously elevated the R&D operation within the company and made it plain that he would be raising his expectations accordingly.

Brunner told me that Smale's remarks "resounded" within the R&D operation at P&G. "It was a huge statement — and boy, talk about energizing. Within the research and development community, man, this was really major."

The company had always spent far more on R&D than its competitors did, Brunner said, but the spending wasn't always focused.

Under Smale, though, R&D operations were tightly integrated into the business units at P&G. Within different divisions, R&D managers were elevated to the level of vice presidents.

"It may not sound like much, but at the time it was a big deal," Brunner explained.

It meant technologists, like him, were now part of the company's executive committee — bringing R&D's voice into the company's most important decisions.

Brunner was one of those first R&D vice presidents, and he recalled being brought in to see Smale.

"He talked about the importance of innovation in the company, how the company never really grew big except for major innovation around new brands or acquisitions. And that he was depending on us, on me, to lead. What was needed was breakthrough products and new brands. And, you know, John was stern. So he said it in a way you didn't forget."

I was beginning to notice a strange duality in how people spoke about Smale. He was revered by many who had worked with him, even beloved. But they also recalled an iciness that I found hard to square with the affection.

The aim of my conversation with A.G. Lafley was somewhat different. He was Smale's junior by 20 years and had relatively little direct contact with him as he worked his way up the ladder. When Lafley became CEO for the first time, in 2000, Smale had been retired for nearly a decade.

One thing I wanted to understand was the lasting impact that Smale had on the company. But first, I got a lesson on what it means to become the CEO of a company with a history like P&G's.

Lafley told me that, when he learned that he was going to be named CEO, he started a personal project.

"I read every single P&G annual shareholders' letter, from the first one in the 1890s, when the company went public, to the present, so I read all of John's letters," he said. "And then as you know, if you've been in the archives, they have collections of all of the talks [CEOs] ever did, externally or internally. And I read every one of those."

He listed the names of past leaders of the business, going back decades, and said, "Far and away, I learned the most from John."

I wanted to ask exactly what he had learned, but I was still doing the mental math. I had been in the archives, and I had seen the collections. I had no reason to doubt that Lafley really had gone over all that material, but I also realized it was a massive undertaking. It made me stop and consider, for just a moment, what taking the reins of P&G must mean to someone who has spent an entire career with the company.

Lafley, meanwhile, had moved on with his discussion. Like Brunner, he recalled the emphasis Smale had placed on innovation.

"One of the cool things about P&G is we were encouraged to make mistakes, to learn from mistakes and learn from failures. Fail early, fail often, fail cheap, and learn from it."

Smale, he said, "was willing to roll the dice on a new innovation or a new technology."

As we spoke, I thought back to Smale's oral history. One section had jumped out to me when I first saw it.

"Any living company has got to have growth," Smale had said. "You've got to be able to offer opportunities for people. The whole reason that you exist is to produce profits for your shareholders, but fundamentally, you don't start with that. You start with people who are motivated to accomplish great things. Almost inevitably that means growth — whether the great thing can be a dentifrice that cuts decay or disposable diapers or what have you — but that's going to result in growth. You're stimulated to invent that better dentifrice because you know, if you do, you're going to have real growth measured by share or shipments. ... What creates the growth are the inventions and the people doing the things that are going to stimulate it."

All this was of a piece with what Lafley was telling me. Eventually, I asked Lafley to boil down what he took away from Smale's shareholder letters and speeches.

"John was, as much as any of us, a man of principle," Lafley began, "and I distinguish that from a man of strategy. If you really look at what he and the leadership team tried to do, in the '80s, they were willing to shift the strategy around and change the strategy when they felt they weren't getting the results that they wanted."

What was the principle?

"We have to grow," Lafley said.

CHAPTER 3

"Even If I Have to Scrub Floors"

As I prepared for my first reporting trip to Cincinnati, I mentioned to my father that I had a new project. The name John Smale definitely rang a bell with him. Likely, it was simply because he'd spent an entire working life focused on the business world and would have paid attention to the business news during Smale's time at P&G and GM.

In conversations with Cathy and through my own research, I had developed a pretty detailed background on Smale. As it turned out, he and my father were both from the same part of the world. My father had grown up in Utica, while Smale was from Listowel, Ontario. If you drew a straight line between the two, each was about 75 miles from Lake Ontario, just on opposite sides of the border. Both were avid fisherman. Both grew up with one sibling, a sister. My father's sister was called Gay, and Smale's, his twin, was named Joy.

Here, though, things diverged. The Smales had left Ontario when the twins were young, and John and Joy grew up in Elmhurst, Ill., just outside Chicago.

Their father, Peter, was a Canadian World War I veteran from Wellesley, Ontario, who worked as a traveling salesman for the wholesale division of the Marshall Field's department store. Peter Smale had an eighth-grade education, but his son would always say his father was the smartest person he had ever known.

Peter Smale traveled across the Midwest for Marshall Field, selling bolts of cloth, woolens and yard goods. It was good, steady work, and it allowed John Smale to grow up in what he later called a "conventional" home at a time when Americans in general couldn't take that for granted.

A few months after Smale's second birthday, the U.S. stock market crashed, and "Black Tuesday" ushered in the Great Depression. Peter Smale's work for Marshall Field continued, nonetheless, and his son would grow up very aware of the difference a steady job at an established company could make for a worker and his family.

By 1940, Peter Smale was earning a respectable $5,000 per year, and the family rented a recently built home on Parkside Avenue in Elmhurst for $60 per month.

While Peter Smale traveled, his wife, Vera, raised the children with an emphasis on academic achievement. Neither parent had attended college, but Vera was determined that their children would do so.

Of the two, Joy Smale was the better student. At York Community High School, John Smale kept himself busy outside of academics, appearing in the school play, editing the school newspaper and joining the debate club.

But Vera never let her son forget her plans for him.

"John," she would frequently remind him, "you are going to college, even if I have to scrub floors to send you."

Smale understood his parents' expectations, but it frustrated him that he had to work harder than his sister to achieve the same results in school. He was plainly as smart as or smarter than his peers, but his grades didn't reflect that, and they seldom matched his sister's.

Once, to motivate his son, Peter made a bargain with his two children. John and Joy had begged for years for a dog. If they both managed to get straight A's in school, Peter said, he would let them have one. It was a promise Peter never thought he would have to keep. He just hoped it would spark an improvement in his son's grades.

But the introduction of a goal turned out to be extremely motivating for John. He buckled down, spending long hours over homework assignments and assigned reading. Joy did her part as well, and at the end of the semester, the twins presented a pair of perfect report cards.

Peter was pleased, but he told the children that he had changed his mind about the dog. Instead of a puppy, he said, he would buy them a typewriter to use for their school assignments.

Smale's youngest daughter, Lisa, told me that her father never forgot the sting from that parental bait-and-switch, passing the story on to his own kids as something that "showed me how not to behave."

It had also shown John something else: If he put in the extra effort, he could perform at the level everyone expected him to. It wasn't clear why he had to put in that extra effort in academics. In other activities, like theater, he was adept at memorizing lines and lyrics. Most things outside the classroom came easily to him.

But it was undeniable that, if he wanted to succeed on the path his parents had set for him, hard work was the key ingredient.

———

Every summer, Vera would take the twins back to Canada. It was there, in the lakes and ponds that dot the rolling farmland of rural Ontario, that John was introduced to fishing. It was his mother who first showed him how to toss a line over the side of a rowboat.

After that, he took every opportunity he could to fish. As he grew older, his mother or an aunt would pack him a sandwich, and Smale would spend his days wandering the woods with a cane pole and a can of worms, planting the seeds of a lifelong passion for the outdoors and, above all, for fishing.

With World War II underway, Smale enlisted in the Navy at age 17, but he had to defer entry until his 18th birthday in August 1945. He was content to finish out his senior year of high school, but his parents had other plans.

Joy had been looking at colleges, and both she and her father had taken a liking to Miami University in Oxford, Ohio. In a conversation with an admissions officer, Peter mentioned that Joy had a twin brother who was headed to the Navy the next year.

By that time, the signs were clear that the war was going to end. The admissions officer warned Peter that, if his son was planning to go to college after the Navy, he might have a hard time getting admitted. A crush of returning veterans was likely to swell classes at colleges and universities across the country.

However, he said, if John were to leave high school early, spend the spring semester at Miami and take summer classes before shipping out to basic training, he'd be guaranteed readmission when he was discharged.

Back home in Elmhurst, the advice made the choice crystal-clear to Vera and Peter.

Under protest, Smale withdrew from high school, and in the winter of 1945, he found himself in Ohio, an unwilling second-semester freshman at Miami University.

When he turned 18 in August, Smale received orders to report for basic training, but first he went back to Oxford to visit friends. While there, he ran into a high school classmate who attended Western College, a nearby women's school. With her was an attractive young redhead from Evansville, Ind., named Phyllis Weaver.

The next day, Smale was walking down High Street in Oxford with his former roommate when he spotted Phyllis across the street with another girl. "I know the redhead," he said. "Why don't we ask them if they'd like to go to the movies?"

"Okay," his friend said. "But I think I'd like to go with the redhead."

Smale reached into his pocket and, pulling out a coin, made the most fateful bet of his life.

"I'll flip you for it," he said.

————

John Smale's career in the Navy was short and unremarkable. He described it once as being spent "for the most part behind the steam table of a galley." One feature of it was his continued pursuit of Phyllis Weaver. After he won the coin toss with his roommate, he exchanged letters with her all through his time in the service.

Cathy told me that John and Phyllis held on to each other's letters for decades. As Phyllis battled the cancer that would take her life in 2006, John would read aloud to her from the letters written 60 years before by a lovesick seaman first class.

After less than a year on active duty, Smale fell gravely ill with pneumonia and was given a medical discharge. By the fall of 1946, he was back at Miami — and back with Phyllis Weaver. They would be a couple throughout their remaining years in school, and by all accounts, Smale remained as smitten as he seemed in his letters.

Years later, when his long-time friend and fellow Miami alumnus Charlie Mechem interviewed him for the school's *Miamian* magazine, Smale would recall the day when he gave Phyllis his Phi Delta Theta fraternity pin.

In keeping with tradition, Smale told Mechem, his entire fraternity marched to the dorm where Phyllis lived to watch Smale stand under her window and serenade her with a solo performance of "I Love You Truly."

————

It was while serving as the Phi Delta Theta social chairman that Smale made one of his first ventures into the world of business.

The responsibility for planning the frat's parties fell to him, and as he was working to come up with unique and enjoyable social events, he realized that at hundreds of schools across the country, an untold number of his fellow social chairs were in a similar position. What if they pooled their collective experience?

He found a listing of all the fraternity and sorority chapters at colleges across the United States and, with the help of Phyllis, drafted a form letter, asking them to share their best party ideas. The responses came streaming back. Smale compiled the best ideas for themed get-togethers and other social events into a booklet, which he titled *Party 'Em Up*, and drafted another form letter. This time, he offered to sell his fellow social chairs the distilled party-planning expertise of hundreds of fraternities and sororities, cash-on-delivery.

The response was so great that he once again enlisted Phyllis to help type up the replies. He asked for her help again the next year with a follow-up version of the booklet, *Party 'Em Up Some More*, which also sold briskly.

The two booklets, along with the G.I. Bill, paid for Smale's final three years at school. They also helped convince him that a product offering people something they'd never had before, something that made their lives easier, practically sold itself.

———

Another experience that stuck with Smale from his time at Miami University was summer work for Oxford Research Associates, a company operated by a marketing professor named Joe Seibert. Smale was paid 40 cents per hour to conduct opinion research and to gather signatures on petitions.

One project was on behalf of a company called NuMaid Margarine. At the time, Ohio law prohibited margarine from being sold with the yellow coloring that made it resemble butter. But without the yellow coloring, a block of margarine looked like lard — not an appealing thing to spread on your morning toast.

NuMaid had addressed the problem by packaging its margarine with a tablet of yellow dye that housewives were expected to massage into the product to change its color. The company knew this was harming sales and hired Oxford to gather signatures for a petition to the legislature to change the law.

Smale had no particular passion for margarine, but he found the job itself stimulating. He enjoyed selling people on the company's cause and was fascinated by the thinking that went into the campaign. There was a problem that made a product less appealing to consumers, and NuMaid had charted a course toward solving it.

Despite the pittance he was being paid to do it — something he complained about in letters home — Smale's introduction to the world of marketing was revelatory.

"That's when I decided what I wanted to do," Smale would later recall. "I wanted to get into marketing."

————

When Smale graduated in the summer of 1949, he took a job with the Vick Chemical Co., which made popular cold and flu remedies. A little over a year later, in September 1950, he and Phyllis were married.

In his time at Vick, Smale often found himself bored. If the world is divided between people who live to work and people who work to live, Smale found he was definitely among the former. The problem, as Smale saw it, was that there wasn't enough work for him to do at Vick, and what there was left little room for independent thought and innovation.

He left Vick before he'd been there two full years, taking a chance on a New York City start-up called The BioResearch Co. Launched by a wealthy entrepreneur, the company was marketing a new kind of nose drops, and Smale was brought on to run test markets in Wisconsin and Illinois.

By 1952, with Phyllis back at her parents' home in Indiana, preparing to give birth to the couple's first child, it was clear that things were going badly for the company's founder. When Phyllis delivered their son, John Jr., in September, Smale handed his paycheck to his father-in-law to pay the hospital bill. The check bounced.

The next day, Smale picked up a copy of the *Chicago Tribune* and saw an advertisement for a brand management job at Procter & Gamble in Cincinnati. He answered it and was invited in for an interview. The next Friday, on the drive back to New York, he detoured to Cincinnati, where he was interviewed and subjected to the battery of tests that P&G gave all of its prospective employees.

On Monday, back in New York, Smale's phone rang. Bill Alexander, then the advertising manager for P&G's Drug Products division, was calling to offer him an assistant brand manager job that paid $450 per month. When could Smale start, Alexander wanted to know. The company would like him to come on board soon. Within three weeks, if possible.

"I'll be there on Wednesday," Smale replied.

At Procter & Gamble, Smale found everything that he had been missing at Vick Chemical Company. There was plenty of work, room for him to take initiative, and the promise of advancement.

By his own account, Smale quickly developed a sense that Procter & Gamble was somehow different from the other companies he had worked for and those that his friends had signed up with out of college.

The organization was filled with people from different backgrounds with different personalities, but they all shared a deeply competitive nature. There was an ethos of "winning" inherent in the organization, he'd later recall, a desire to be the best at whatever one was doing.

Smale bought in to the company's culture of intensive work and intolerance for mediocrity, and modeled himself on the leaders he saw at the top of the organization.

The P&G culture the company's leaders sought to pass down to a new generation of executives went beyond a strong work ethic and the desire to win, though. The implicit message was that the company was led by people of good character.

In a year-end speech shortly after Smale was hired, then-president Neil McElroy pledged to the company's assembled employees, "Procter will never ask you to do anything that you can't discuss with your wife and children at the breakfast table."

In an interview three decades later, Smale would discuss the impact that kind of leadership has on a new employee.

"When young people join an organization, certainly a lot of their character has been formed, but the company, their environment, also has a role to play in the formation of their character. If you start in an association when you're 21, 22, or 23 years old, you are still being molded in how you think about life."

It certainly appeared to have an effect on Smale. People who knew him at the time told me that, in the office at P&G, he seemed to be cast from the same mold as the company's top leaders: focused, unsmiling, almost severe. The message his demeanor sent to both his colleagues and superiors was that he was a serious man who ought to be taken seriously.

Outside the office, though, there was a side to Smale that his coworkers didn't necessarily get to see.

The Smale family was growing. Cathy was born a couple of years after John, Jr., and was followed by another daughter, Lisa, and a second son, Peter, a few years later.

The Smale's oldest son, who goes by Jay, told me that after his parents moved the family to the Terrace Park neighborhood east of downtown Cincinnati, his father earned a reputation for organizing themed parties, and for being a bit of a prankster.

No doubt drawing on expertise gained from *Party 'Em Up*, he once rented gambling tables and handed guests $5,000 in play money to spend on dice and card games in the Smale's house. Another time, he rented the Terrace Park Community Center and created an indoor "horse race," again doling out play money to partygoers and having them bet on horses, which advanced with the roll of a pair of dice.

When his friend and next-door neighbor, Fred Gronville, turned 40, the slightly younger Smale had a huge sign printed and hung above his neighbor's front door announcing the birthday.

Later that day, Jay told me, Gronville sought some escape at the Terrace Park community swimming pool. As he lay relaxing in the sun, the pool's loudspeakers crackled to life, and Smale's voice rang out across the entire complex. He had called in from home and convinced the manager to patch him through to the speaker system.

"Attention please!" Smale said. "We have a special announcement: Fred Gronville is now 40 years old!" He then led the entire crowd at the pool in singing "Happy Birthday" to his mortified neighbor.

CHAPTER 4

To the Best of Your Ability, Do the Right Thing

I was supposed to meet Bob Wehling, the retired global marketing officer of Procter & Gamble, at the Queen City Club on a Sunday morning. I had arrived a few minutes early and, to my annoyance, found myself standing in the rain facing a locked door. I could tell there were people inside, but nobody seemed interested in letting me in.

As I stood there getting wet, Wehling turned the corner and mounted the steps. Someone promptly unlocked the door and ushered the two of us in. Membership has its privileges, I guess.

Wehling had spent 40 years at Procter & Gamble, a career that earned him a place in the American Advertising Federation's Hall of Fame, but he didn't want to talk to me about P&G's big successes on his watch. He wanted to tell me about the time John Smale took a chance on an extremely unlikely job applicant.

It was early 1960, Wehling told me, and he was looking — somewhat desperately — for a job. Despite a résumé that offered little more than a bachelor's degree in English, the young father, with a second child on the way, had talked his way into an interview for an advertising job with Procter & Gamble.

"John was my interviewer," Wehling told me. "And the first question he asked me was, what did I think of *Printers' Ink* magazine?"

Printers' Ink was an advertising industry trade publication that would have been familiar to almost anybody in the business.

"I said I'd never heard of it. And then he asked me several more business- and advertising-related questions. And I had no idea. He said, 'Well, if you don't know anything about advertising, why did you apply for an advertising job?'" Wehling laughed.

"I said I just recently read a novel about advertising, and it sounded like it would be interesting," he continued. "And the other reason I applied is because I have a wife and child, and another one on the way, and I need a job."

At this point, he said, Smale was shaking his head in disbelief.

"He said, 'Well, give me one good reason why I should offer you a job.' And I said, 'Because I'll work harder than anybody else.' And he said, 'Well ... I like that.'"

Wehling got the job and kept his promise, working the same grueling hours that Smale put in — early mornings, late nights, and weekends. He moved through several promotions in the health and beauty care part of the P&G business before getting word one day that he was being transferred to the Paper Products division to help the tissue brand Puffs in its perpetual struggle to best Kleenex.

"I didn't want to move out of the health and beauty care business to paper," Wehling said. "I told them, I thought I'd look for another job in the health and beauty care business somewhere. And that led to a meeting with John Smale and his boss. And he said something to me in that meeting that tells you a lot about John. He said, 'No matter where you work, sooner or later, you're going to have to learn to trust somebody. And we want to be the ones you trust. Trust us.'"

Smale told him that he knew Wehling really wanted to be the brand manager for Crest — the marquee brand in the Health and Beauty Care division. "But," Smale said, "you know, we need [Puffs] to grow. You do that, and we'll watch over you."

A year and a half later, Smale made good on his promise: Wehling was running Crest.

As the interview wound down, Wehling said he had one more thing he wanted to mention. He began talking about P&G's relationship with its advertising agencies and how occasionally, it became necessary for the company to terminate those relationships.

"John's point of view was always that that should only be a last resort. And if you have to do it, you have to do it humanely and carefully. I always got advice from him when we had a difficult agency situation, and it all got handled in a way that was very professional. In another company, that doesn't always happen that way."

I was genuinely puzzled as to why he was bringing this up.

"Help me understand why that's important," I said.

"One, you never know what's going to happen in the future, and you could wind up needing the people again," he said.

But there was something even more important. "John wanted to be very sure that, if we were terminating a relationship, or in other words, penalizing an agency, that it really was the agency's fault. There are a lot of people, even in [P&G], who whenever something went wrong, they'd blame the agency, even though it was our fault. And John knew that ... and he wanted to make sure that wasn't the case. So that we could live with ourselves."

That was an odd thing to say, I thought. I couldn't imagine many people had trouble living with themselves after terminating an ad contract.

But Wehling was adamant. "The way he phrased it to me, and I have always phrased it to the people who work for me, was you should always try, to the best of your ability, to do the right thing. The right thing in any situation. The right thing for a consumer, the right thing for a retailer, the right thing for your shareholders, the right thing for the people who work for you. If you can tell yourself that, to the best of your ability, you tried to do the right thing, you would always be okay. I mean, not everybody would agree with it. But you could live with yourself and feel good about things."

It wasn't the first time I had heard the phrase "do the right thing" in connection with Smale or P&G. In fact, it's virtually impossible to spend any time with people steeped in the P&G culture without their reminding you that phrase was the company's unofficial motto.

I had usually brushed it off as a bit of corporate puffery — something people said to signal that they had bought in to the company's self-propagated public image. But listening to Wehling talk about how he and Smale sweated the details of canceling an ad contract made me wonder whether there was more to it than I had thought.

CHAPTER 5

Smale's Safety Valve

Early in my research, it became obvious that it would be impossible to write about John Smale without writing about fishing. After P&G and Phyllis, it was his great passion, one that he tried, and mostly failed, to pass on to his children.

Smale, in a 1993 interview, described fishing as a "safety valve" that, even when he wasn't on the water, gave him respite from worries about work.

"If I wake at 2 or 3 in the morning worried about a business issue, to which I don't have a solution, I'll think back to incidents that I can visualize," he said. "I guess golfers can visualize great moments when a ball was hit just so, when they felt themselves cast across the course. Well, I have a mental image of a fish, a seven-pound salmon. I can see that fish about as clearly today as I could the day after I ate it. I can still see that fish coming back to the fly. And other incidents like that, it's a way to get my mind off the things that bother me, that I no longer want to chew. And when I'm out there on the river, I never think about business; I'm totally engrossed. I can be standing, casting off the platform of a skiff looking for bonefish ... and I can be doing that for hours ... not seeing anything, and I'm still not thinking about business. I'm still focused on the fish."

It made me think of the countless hours my siblings and I had spent with our father, fishing from a canoe on the Delaware River. It wasn't until I was older that I came to understand that those trips, which began before sunrise and ended with us trudging home, exhausted and sunburned, well after dinner time, had been *his* safety valve, taking him away, at least for a time, from the pressures of his job.

While Smale's passion for fishing hadn't been inherited by his children, his grandson Chris Caldemeyer, Cathy's son, had received a full dose.

Chris teaches creative writing at a private school outside Cincinnati, and he told me that his grandfather had noticed his early interest in fishing, and had cultivated it for years, putting a makeshift rod in his hands when he was in preschool.

Chris told me that he still has the stick, with a piece of yarn attached, that his grandfather used to teach him the basics of fly-casting as a small boy.

As we sat in the open-air restaurant on the roof of the Queen City Club, Chris was listing off some of the rivers he had fished with his grandfather. The Miramichi in New Brunswick, the Cascapédia in Quebec, and others.

The names were familiar to me. Though I had never fished them, I knew that my father had. These were mostly private reserves, where fishing was limited and happened by invitation only. My father's banking connections in New York had occasionally scored him a spot on trips to places he would otherwise never have seen.

Then Chris began mentioning people his grandfather had fished with, and a name leapt out at me.

"Paul Fitzgerald?" I said, a little incredulous. "Your grandfather was friends with Paul Fitzgerald?"

My thoughts went immediately to a thin, dapper man at my father's retirement party. Fitzgerald and my father had worked for the same bank in New York for years and had fished together many times. Fitzgerald was in the business development part of the private bank, and that often involved organizing trips for potential clients to places like the Cascapédia or the Miramichi. When Dad got the chance to visit one of those, it was always because Fitzgerald had found him a slot.

That same evening, I learned that, like my father, Smale had been a member of the Anglers' Club of New York, a by-invitation-only lunch club in the city's

Financial District. Those invitations weren't normally extended to young teachers in Southern Ohio, but Chris mentioned to me that he was a member.

"I have no business being a member of that club," he said with a laugh. But every time he considers letting his membership lapse, he thinks about his grandfather, and so he hangs onto it.

Chris Caldemeyer would wind up being a key touchstone as I worked toward an understanding of who John Smale had been.

Chris had been born while Smale was CEO of Procter & Gamble, but by the time he was old enough to really form a relationship with his grandfather, Smale's time on the stage of corporate America was coming to an end.

Their shared love of fishing gave Chris the opportunity to experience his grandfather in ways that almost nobody else in Smale's family ever would, and it provided insights into his character that I wouldn't find anywhere else.

The uniqueness of their relationship was something that Chris recognized, too, as I would discover in a letter he had written to his grandfather, one that Smale had saved.

Reflecting on their shared fishing trips, Chris wrote, "It was during our time together, that I felt like our friendship blossomed beyond the restrictive bonds of grandfather and grandchild. I don't know about you, and perhaps you never knew this, but I was given the chance to get to know you better than I think many people in our family do, to see the John Smale away from the board room and the dinner table. And I genuinely feel lucky because of that."

––––––––––

That letter brought to mind one of my favorite pictures of my father. On his 70th birthday, my siblings, our spouses, and my parents' eight grandchildren had all descended on my sister's house on the Pennsylvania side of the Delaware River. The whole clan was there to go fishing with Granddad.

A picture from that day shows my father, surrounded by his grandkids, from ages 2 to 12. All are clutching fishing poles, with many standing barefoot on the muddy riverbank.

My father kept it and other pictures from that day on his computer. He labeled the folder "Best 70th Birthday Celebration Ever."

That day was especially meaningful to him because it was something that his own father had never been able to experience.

My paternal grandfather had died of cancer in his 40s, when my father was just a boy, and Dad spent much of his life haunted by that.

It wasn't just the specter of a disease that he worried might someday take him as well. What really troubled him was his knowledge that his sister, two years younger than he was, had grown up with no real memory of their father at all.

As his children grew and had children of their own, Dad had done his best to make sure that they knew who he was. One of the ways he did that was by taking us fishing. He had a picture of the first fish ever caught by each of his children and grandchildren.

The next time I spoke with my father, I mentioned to him that John Smale had been friends with Paul Fitzgerald and, like him, had been a member of the Anglers Club. He found it amusing, but not surprising. The world of serious fly fishermen isn't huge, he said, so it made sense that the two might have had some friends in common.

CHAPTER 6

Great Institutions Have a Soul

One thing that bothered me in the early months of researching John Smale's life was that I had virtually never heard his voice. I had reams of speeches and letters, but only once had I actually heard him speak.

Sitting in the office of Kathy Fish, then P&G's chief technology officer, I watched a brief video that gets played every year when the company announces the winner of the John G. Smale Innovation award. It's a prize that Smale endowed, with a grant of his stock in the company, to highlight the work of an up-and-coming technologist.

The voice in the video fit the image of the man, deep and earnest-sounding, with a slight midwestern accent befitting someone raised outside, but not in, Chicago.

"It's important that the people in R&D understand the enormous importance of what they do, because it really is everything we are," Smale says in the video. He referred to "a fundamental principle I don't think is going to change, and hasn't changed in our history — and that is that we are an R&D-based company. We're a company whose progress and fortunes are based on the success of inventing new brands, new processes that are really distinctive — that are market changers and really revolutionize a market when we go into it.

"Fundamentally, this is an R&D company. If this company is going to be successful 50 years from now, it will be successful for the same reason that it is now, and that's because we are ahead of the world in almost every category and product innovation."

Fish stopped the video. "So, it's funny," she said. "We give the Smale Award to our young innovators every year, and we show this video every year. And every time everybody's so inspired by it. Every time."

———————

Back home, going over my notes from my interview, I thought it was a shame that I didn't have more recordings of Smale. Many people had told me how meaningful his speeches had been to them, and I wished I could listen to some myself.

Some weeks later, UPS delivered a box to my doorstep. I quickly saw that it was from Cathy, but I had no idea what it was. Lugging it into my office, I opened it to find dozens and dozens of CD jewel cases. As I sorted through them, I realized that they were recordings of Smale's various appearances as CEO of Procter & Gamble.

There was everything from annual meeting speeches to Smale delivering opening remarks before a performance by the Ringling Bros. and Barnum & Bailey Circus that the company had sponsored for P&G employees and their kids.

I recalled that Cathy had made a passing remark during one of our interviews that she would send me some recordings, but I had forgotten about it and had no idea just how many there were.

One of the first recordings I grabbed was a series of interviews that Smale did with a team of researchers from General Motors. The videos, which stretched over four hours, had been conducted over two days in October 1999, in Smale's office in Cincinnati.

The object of the interview was to get Smale to open up about his philosophy of management, but the discussion was wide-ranging, covering his early years at P&G right through the end of his time at General Motors.

One of the interviewers asked Smale to repeat a story that he had told in a speech to GM executives. It involved a time when Smale had suffered a rare failure in his work at P&G, in an effort to halt the passage of legislation that the company believed was both unnecessary and harmful to the business.

"The head of the business, Ed Harness, came into my office, and I felt very badly because I felt I'd failed the company in getting this thing done. And I kind of blurted out to him, 'You know, Ed, I love this company.'"

Smale immediately regretted his words, he said. "I thought, 'That's kind of a dumb thing to have said.' How can an individual have that kind of affection for an institution, bricks and mortar and so forth?"

But, he explained, the more he thought about it, the more he understood the gut reaction that led him to say that:

"All institutions like this, and certainly this is true with General Motors, represent more than that. They have a soul. I think, if they're worth anything, they represent a character, they have an ethos. They perpetuate themselves, if they're really well-grounded in their character. They don't depend on the personality of a given leader at a given point in time. They go through decades or generations of leaders. And they do well, I think primarily because, they have, as a foundation, a character that allows people, encourages people, to really dedicate a working life to them, to the fortunes of the company. They feel badly when the company doesn't do well, and they feel great when the company does do well."

I had read similar things in some of Smale's speeches, but hearing him say this out loud felt different. There was an earnestness in his voice that didn't come across on the printed page, and it was all the more affecting, because I had to assume Smale knew these recordings were destined for an archive and probably wouldn't be widely distributed.

The interviewers asked Smale about a business accounting scandal that was being widely covered in the news at the time. How, they asked, could companies inoculate themselves against that kind of behavior by senior management?

"You really have to depend on the fundamental character of the company, and of the people managing the company," Smale said. "And the character of the people managing the company is itself a reflection, or should be a reflection, of the character of the company."

At P&G, Smale explained, the policy was to always promote from within. One of the main reasons the company tried to stick to that policy was that, by the time an executive was in a position to do something like falsify an earnings report, he or she would have been steeped in the company's culture for so long that doing such a thing would be unthinkable.

"You're not picking somebody off the street and confronting them for the first time with the idea that, unless you do such and such, you're going to not make your quarterly earnings and the Street's going to punish you by dropping the stock five or 10 points," he said. "You're talking to somebody who has got the background, hopefully, of a series of generations of tough decisions that were made the right way. So that when they think about that, and the pain that it's going to cause to come out with quarterly earnings that don't match what the Street's telling the investors, they've got that background. They can lean on all of that history and say, 'No, the right thing to do here is not trying to fiddle these earnings but to face up to it.'"

I recalled John Pepper telling me about the time Smale immediately refused the suggestion that P&G withhold marketing support from three new products in order to show an earnings increase in 1985.

That was exactly what Smale was talking about. It would be years before Pepper was in a position to make a similar call, but because he had seen Smale make that tough decision, he had that experience to fall back on when he became CEO.

"That's the kind of thing in an organization that gets passed on," Smale said. "Not through something that's on a piece of paper but through actions, through comments, through statements, so that the younger people in an organization grow up understanding the right way to make a decision is to face up to the truth and not try to cover it one way or another. That is character that's created over time. By actions. By people. By the management."

The interviewers asked Smale about what he saw as P&G's "vision." It was an odd question, I thought, but Smale's answer was interesting.

"Well, P&G's vision, I guess, has really been kind of a simple one for all of the years I've been involved," he said. "It's importantly rooted in character and, as we say often here, doing what's right."

There it was again.

For weeks, I had been going back and forth with Cathy and John Pepper about what the book ought to look like. In the end, we roughed out a structure that would focus almost exclusively on Smale's years as CEO. There would be a certain amount of background, of course, but the plan was not to produce something that looked like a full biography. It was, instead, going to be a highly detailed look at Procter & Gamble during the nine full years that Smale ran the place and at Smale's years at GM.

I already had an ending in mind — letting Smale step offstage with remarks he delivered in 1995, on the occasion of his departure from P&G's board of directors.

"I believe the fundamental responsibility of this management — and of the board of Procter & Gamble — is the successful perpetuation of this institution," he said. "Managers — and directors — will come and go. Shareholders will change. Certainly the world in which we exist will change. We'll have good years of business growth and some that won't be so good. The things that must not change are the basic principles of this company. Those precepts that are articulated in our Statement of Purpose. By following these principles, this company has grown, and its employees and shareholders have profited. ... I'm confident this generation of management and directors will continue to follow these principles. And all the rest — as it has in the past — will follow."

I developed a detailed outline of different chapters of the book. One would focus on the company's many years of struggle to find a way to compete in Japan. Another would focus on how Smale had restructured P&G internally, as part of a relentless effort to push decision-making in the company down through the system — dispersing authority that had, over decades, become too concentrated with senior management.

Other chapters would chronicle the explosive growth of the company after the Richardson-Vicks purchase turned it into a global firm, and again after an alliance with Walmart that rewrote the rules for how all consumer packaged-goods companies interacted with major retailers.

The outline encouraged me. I could see the shape of the final product, and I set about gathering the raw materials I needed to build it.

CHAPTER 7

"You Don't Have the Whole Man"

In October, I traveled to New York to interview Smale's close friend, Ed Artzt, who succeeded him as CEO of P&G. I arrived a day early, and that afternoon, my father called and said he and my mother wanted to have dinner with me. I thought it was odd for them to take the train into the city and then work their way a couple of dozen blocks up to midtown just for dinner. I agreed, but not without a little concern.

It had been a few months since I had last seen my father, and his further weight loss was impossible to miss. The three of us walked a few blocks down 56th Street to Patsy's, an old-school white-tablecloth Italian restaurant that had been open since World War II.

We had an enjoyable dinner, and my concern that I was about to get some bad news slowly dissipated. Apparently, they just wanted to have dinner with one of their kids.

On the sidewalk outside, I hugged my mother goodbye and turned to my father. As my arms wrapped around him, I could feel the coat he was wearing over his sport jacket collapse inward until, at last, I found him. It felt like hugging a boy in his father's clothes.

Six weeks later, Mom and Dad would visit my family for Thanksgiving. My father had lost still more weight. His pants were bunching at the waist under his tightened belt, and his shirt hung loosely from his shoulders.

More worrisome, though, was his constant sniffle and an unexplained cough and shortness of breath. Just three years earlier, he and my mother had hiked part of the Camino de Santiago, logging 15-to-18-mile days over dusty hilltops in Northern Spain, my father toting a heavy camera bag. That Thanksgiving, though, he had struggled walking in a five-mile "Turkey Trot" through the flat, paved streets of Alexandria, Va.

My brother, my two sisters, my brother-in-law and I began having quiet, worried conversations about the next year's fishing trips. The loss of muscle and stamina made it obvious — to us, if not to Dad — that wading in the Ausable or any river with a strong current would be terribly dangerous for him.

———————

The morning after dinner with my parents, I made my way across Central Park and up Park Avenue to Ed Artzt's apartment.

I didn't know what to expect. Artzt, in his time at P&G, had been known as a force of nature. Volcanic of temper and sharp of tongue, he was also brilliant, relentlessly hard-working and fiercely dedicated to P&G as an institution.

However, Artzt was now 89 years old, had Parkinson's disease and was recovering from a fall that had put him in a wheelchair.

I was meeting John Pepper and Shane Meeker, the P&G historian, at the apartment. The day was to begin with the two of them taking an oral history from Artzt, covering his time at P&G. Only afterward would the interview about John Smale commence. I worried that the first interview would take up most of Artzt's energy, and I resigned myself to the likelihood that I wouldn't get much from him that day.

A uniformed doorman escorted me inside the building and handed me off to a similarly uniformed elevator operator, who accompanied me up to Artzt's apartment. Artzt's wife, the art collector Marlies Hessel, greeted me with her singular German-via-Mexico accent and led me into a dining room dominated by "Deep Water," an immersive and colorful floor-to-ceiling installation by the artist Judy Pfaff.

I would not have thought it possible for an 89-year-old man in a wheelchair to give off the impression of strength, but sitting at the head of the table in that dining room, Artzt managed it. His voice was low but powerful, his recall was sharp, and he proceeded to demolish my concerns about his stamina by sitting for 6½ hours of interviews that morning and afternoon, continuing straight through lunch.

———

When Ed Artzt talks about Procter & Gamble, the result is something between a personal reminiscence and a history lesson. When he joined the company, R.R. Deupree was still the chairman, and Deupree had joined the company in 1905, when William A. Procter, the son of the founder, was still in charge.

One of the things Artzt did that day was describe for us a ritual that he and Smale had both participated in as young members of the executive team in the 1960s.

Every day, he said, the entire administrative committee — the heads of businesses and of staff operations — were expected to attend lunch on the 11th floor of P&G's headquarters building, where the company's most senior executives had their offices.

Deupree, though long retired, sat at the head of the table. Howard Morgens, the CEO, and Neil McElroy, the chairman of the board, sat at the corners to either side of him. The pattern was the same every day. One of the men at the head of the table would set out a topic for discussion. It might be a particular business issue the company was facing, or an action being considered by the government, or another topic relevant to P&G.

The conversation would begin, normally among Deupree, Morgens and McElroy, with more junior attendees only speaking if they were invited to do so. Even the most senior members of the executive committee, like Ed Harness, already seen as a likely successor to Morgens, rarely interrupted. And they certainly never tried to steer the conversation away from the topic of the day, chosen by the men at the head of the table.

Through those lunches, day after day and year upon year, Artzt said, he and Smale absorbed the lessons accumulated by generations of the company's managers.

Deupree had joined the company as a clerk. He became an officer of the firm under the leadership of William Cooper Procter, who in the late 1800s had persuaded the company's management to give employees Saturday afternoons off with pay, and later, to implement a profit-sharing plan. Both were unheard of at the time.

By the time Smale and Artzt sat down in those daily lunches, Deupree had more than 50 years of insights into management of the company.

In my research, I came across the text of remarks Deupree made to the Alumni Conference of the Harvard Business School in 1948. He had articulated a key insight that he and others would pass down to future leaders of the company — a lesson that, I now knew, had resonated deeply with Smale. It was that management was responsible to its employees — not just its shareholders — to run a profitable enterprise:

> To me, the first responsibility of management to its employees is to operate a successful business — a business which makes a profit. I mean a regular, healthy profit, the kind that continues to pay wages and expand a business, thereby making new jobs. ... Profits are the lifeblood of a business and of the continuing progress of the individuals in the business. There could be no business expansion, no industrial progress without profits. As for real benefits to employees, just try to find them in a firm which makes no profits.

Inextricably linked to that drive to run a profitable business, Deupree continued, was a commitment to providing opportunities for employees to grow and advance. It was vital, he said:

... to give the individual employee a chance to develop the best that is in him. This may sound like a platitude. It is not. Select a man carefully for the job he is going to fill. Give him proper training and supervision. Then give that man a real chance to prove his ability, to earn money. ... If the worker is confident he will be paid according to his ability to produce, you help him and help his production. As he sees himself doing a better job, he gains pride in his work and confidence in himself. The conditions in his home tend to reflect his increased earnings, and you have a much better employee and citizen. Self-respecting employees make the kind of Americans who are active and eager to serve in their communities.

That speech and my conversation with Artzt made it easy to see the through-line between the company's founders and the people running it generations later.

At one point in our conversation, Artzt noted that P&G had preserved little of the words and writing of its original founders. The company's culture and expectations were passed down through the years by example and discussion.

But he reminded me of one phrase, attributed to James Gamble, that had survived and become something of a mantra for the company's leadership: "If you cannot make pure goods and full weight, go to something else that is honest, even if it is breaking stone."

––––––––––

John Pepper and I sat for nearly an hour listening to Artzt talk about the series of steps he and Smale had taken in the 1980s to turn P&G into a truly global company.

"He had a vision of things like that that was kind of above everybody else's," Artzt said. "He could see things that we were all maybe too busy to see. Or maybe we didn't have his maturity of vision."

But he also described a person very focused on specific results and holding people to account. A key to success, Artzt said, was that business units needed the right leadership or, as Smale put it, they had to be "right at the top."

That meant something very specific, Artzt explained. "It means you've got a person who knows what to do, not just how to do it." It was the distinction between "implementers" — people who could get a job done — and those who understood what job to focus on in the first place.

"John was a great believer, I know, in trying to search out people who could think well enough to know what to do — and not just how to do it — when an issue was in front of them," Artzt told me. "He said, 'We don't pay enough attention to the importance of that question when the time comes to evaluate people. Does that person know what to do when faced with a bunch of consequential options?' It's probably one of the most important things that John taught me over the years. And he was very tough about that. Very tough. If he thought somebody didn't really know what to do in a tough situation, he would really insist on replacing or moving them to a lesser job. He was not willing to tolerate that."

Artzt's comment made me think of a speech Smale had delivered in Cincinnati after his retirement from P&G. He told the story of Dwight Eisenhower's decision to fire his old friend Maj. Gen. Lloyd Fredendall after a disastrous defeat at the Kasserine Pass in Tunisia in 1943.

"Eisenhower had no qualms about demoting his old friend," Smale had said approvingly. "Boldness and swiftness were understood to be the order of the day."

After Pepper left, Artzt's tone shifted slightly:

"The thing I wanted to stress with you is that John Smale and I had a very special relationship. We were very close as we worked together over those 10 years, building something that had never been built before in the company. I think to him it was one of the important achievements of his tenure, as it was for me, too."

It seemed important to him to convey the bond he had shared with Smale.

"John and I spent a lot of time together, after work, and during work, in the late evening," he said.

"Socially?"

"Yeah, socially, but that's not what I'm talking about. I'm talking about going over the business, going over the organization, talking about people," Artzt said.

"He would share with me his feelings about all the people reporting to him as well as the people reporting to me. He was very open with me, and I was privileged to be included in his thinking, so he could bounce things off of somebody. There weren't too many people he could do that with."

We were now well past the six-hour mark, and Artzt and I agreed to meet again in the future to resume our discussion. I was packing my bag when he began talking again. I reached into my bag and flicked my recorder back on.

He started listing the names of every person who had run Procter & Gamble before he did, dating back to 1930, when R.R. Deupree took over. Artzt had personally known all of them and had worked under all but Deupree.

"John was the best of the bunch," Artzt said. "He was. I couldn't have wanted a better guy to work for."

This was the third former CEO of P&G to tell me that Smale was the best CEO he had ever known.

Within the next few weeks, I would speak to other former P&G chief executives. All of them spoke of Smale in superlatives—as someone they not only respected but admired. P&G executives who had left the company and become CEOs elsewhere told me they modeled themselves on him.

I'd interviewed a lot of businesspeople over the years, CEOs, founders, and the like. I couldn't remember a time when I'd had them lining up to tell me how remarkable someone else's leadership was.

———

A few weeks later, I returned to New York to sit with Artzt again, and this time he told me something that I hadn't known: He had never expected to become CEO of Procter & Gamble.

That seemed odd — even unbelievable. Everything I knew about the company's history told me that up-and-coming CEOs were identified, practically if not publicly, years in advance of their actual nominations. And Artzt, in particular, seemed tailor-made for the job.

Running P&G's international business, Artzt had overseen a vast expansion of the company into dozens of countries, building operations on five different continents. Under his watch in the 1980s, income from overseas business had more than doubled, from $3.2 billion per year to $8.5 billion, and it now made up 40% of P&G's overall revenue. On top of that success, Artzt had worked in virtually every part of P&G over nearly 40 years. It was hard to imagine a person more qualified to be the company's CEO.

The problem wasn't qualifications, Artzt explained. It was simple math.

Traditionally, Procter & Gamble CEOs had never stayed on past the age of 63. There was no formal rule — just long-standing tradition. There was also no formal rule about the age at which a person could be appointed CEO, yet the company's board had historically looked for someone in their forties or fifties to take on the highly demanding task. Morgens had taken over the company at age 47, Harness at 56 and Smale at 54.

Artzt was nearly three years younger than Smale. If Smale stayed on until he was 63, Artzt would already be 60. If Smale broke tradition and stayed on to 65 — and given the company's booming profits, there would likely be no opposition if he did — Artzt would be 62. In either case, he would likely be considered too old to take Smale's place.

Artzt told me the writing had been on the wall since the late 1970s, when it became clear that Smale would succeed Harness. In the intervening years, Artzt had been offered opportunities to leave P&G and run other businesses himself, but he had never been interested.

"I wanted to stay at P&G," he said. "I liked what I was doing, and I liked where I was. I didn't want to go into some unknown situation just to get another stripe on my shoulder."

It wasn't something he and Smale spoke about, he told me; there was nothing to say. But one day in 1989, Smale did query Artzt about his plans for the future.

"He said, 'What are you thinking about for retirement?' And I had done a lot of thinking about it," Artzt told me. "And I said, 'John, it's very simple. I'm here for the duration. As long as you're running the business. When you leave, I leave. And it doesn't matter when that is.'"

"Thank you, Ed," Smale said. "Thanks. I appreciate it."

And that, as far as Artzt knew, was the end of the conversation. Until one night in October 1989, when he was about to board the P&G plane for a flight back to Cincinnati. He called his secretary to check in, and she told him that Smale wanted to speak with him.

"Ed, when are you getting in?" Smale asked. "Could we meet at the hangar when you get here?"

Artzt's immediate thought was that something bad had happened to his wife or children. Smale never came out to the airport to see him. There was no need; Lunken Airport was less than 15 minutes away from P&G headquarters.

"John, is there bad news about my family?" Artzt said.

"Oh, no, no, no. It's nothing like that," Smale said quickly. "I just need to talk to you. So, if you could, let's meet at the hangar when you come in."

Artzt was so relieved that he didn't give it much more thought during his flight back home. The airport was mostly dark and empty when the plane touched down, but the two men found a room in the hangar and sat down.

Smale wasted no time: "Ed, I've decided that it's time for me to move on, and the board has decided to elect you as my successor, as chairman and CEO of the company."

"I really was completely taken by it," Artzt told me. "I wasn't expecting it, I wasn't demanding it, I wasn't looking forward to it. I'd sort of made my peace."

He would later piece together that Smale had spoken to the board that day and had the directors sign off on making Artzt his replacement. He had insisted on meeting at the airport because he knew it was likely that, when Artzt got home, he'd start getting congratulatory phone calls from board members. Smale wanted Artzt to hear it from him personally and thought, rightly, that was the way Artzt would prefer things as well.

Artzt struggled to process what had just happened. It had been well over a decade since he'd accepted that becoming CEO wasn't in his future.

"I'm doing this for your sake," Smale said. "I'm doing this so that you can have a run at it. Long enough to take the company where you think it should go."

I had wondered why Smale chose to retire at 62, just as everything he had put in place at P&G was coming to fruition. Now I had my answer.

"He deserved to stay on through age 65 if he wanted to," Artzt said. "And the fact that he deserved to stay on and still went out at 62 is an example of what kind of a human being he was."

"How did that make you feel?" I asked him.

"Grateful," he said.

Across my hours of conversations with Artzt, I ticked through things I wanted to cover with him: Smale's philosophy of management; his process for strategic decision-making; how he approached tricky personnel questions.

In the back of my mind, I had that chapter outline. There were specific things I needed answers to and information about. I needed to check all of those boxes.

When we wrapped up one of our sessions together and I was gathering my things, he stopped me and said, "Let me make a suggestion."

I braced myself, because I knew what was coming. I was about to get writing advice.

It doesn't always happen, but it's not uncommon in my profession for people who are inevitably going to be part of the story you're working on to try to shape the way it gets told.

I typically respond poorly to this sort of thing. I don't get angry or loud, but I immediately snap into a frame of mind in which I assume everything I'm about to hear is wrong, self-serving and unworthy of serious consideration. It's not reasonable, or even logical — it's just a visceral reaction I get to people telling me that, effectively, they know how to do my job better than I do.

But I was wrong. Artzt didn't want to give me writing advice, exactly. It was more like reporting advice. And his tone wasn't peremptory. It was almost pleading.

"What I hear from you today is a lot of this serious stuff that John explained and expressed," he said. "In other words, you want to know what this guy believed in? Here are the things he believed in. And you covered that very well. But I think you need to get more of what this guy was like as an individual that made him so well-liked by the people that really knew him. There's another side to John that's worth exploring. John had a very human-touch side about him, and he was fun to be with."

Out on the sidewalk, I stewed over what Artzt had said. What he was telling me was that, in my reporting on Smale, he thought I had the CEO but I didn't have the man.

Artzt had hit a nerve. By that time, I had learned about as much about John Smale's career as I could. I had cataloged his accomplishments and successes to a level of detail that, if I let it, could have filled two books.

Now I feared that I was missing something central to the story.

I couldn't have articulated it at the time, but over the coming months, I would be forced to understand what it meant to try to sum up a man's life. And I would learn what a mistake I had made in thinking it could be boiled down to the highlights of a business career.

PART TWO

CHAPTER 8

A Grim Coincidence

In the winter of 2019, my father's condition began to get worse. Doctors ran tests to see if the heart problems that had led to his bypass surgery two years earlier had returned, but they found nothing alarming about his heart.

At Christmas, he mentioned another trip to the Ausable in the spring. We all nodded and said we'd keep a weekend open. But we were becoming convinced that there was no way that Dad could wade there, or almost anywhere, safely.

In January, I was drafting a chapter of the book when I received a call from my parents — unusually, during the workday. Normally we spoke in the evening. They were calling to tell me that Dad had been to a pulmonologist to have his lungs examined.

The news was not good. He had been tentatively diagnosed with a degenerative condition that had already left considerable scarring on both of his lungs. The damage wasn't reversible, and the progress of the disease couldn't be stopped. The only hope was to slow it down.

I sat down and wrote a note to Cathy, telling her that the chapter was going to be delayed by a couple of days. Without going into detail, I said that my father had been diagnosed with an obscure degenerative lung condition and that the family was trying to process things.

She wrote me back almost immediately, "I'm so sorry to hear that. My father suffered from pulmonary fibrosis, which ultimately took his life."

I stared at the screen for a few moments in shock. I had known Smale died of a lung condition, but I had been focused on researching his years at P&G and hadn't yet focused on the last years of his life. Dad's diagnosis was idiopathic pulmonary fibrosis. I was writing a book about a man who died from the same disease that was killing my father.

———

A few weeks after learning about Dad's condition, I drove up to my parents' home in New Jersey for a follow-up appointment with the pulmonologist.

On the way to the appointment, my father seemed nervous and distracted. My mother had always found it incredibly difficult to get him to go to the doctor. As a boy of 9, he had watched his father die of cancer, and in his early 20s, he had lost his mother, also to cancer. For most of his life, he'd taken it as a certainty that cancer would, one day, come for him, and he didn't want to hear the news.

Turning the radio on for distraction, we heard that travelers from China, where a dangerous new coronavirus was devastating whole regions of the country, were being quarantined in the United States. So far, just 11 cases of the disease had been identified in America, but the assumption was that it was already spreading.

Soon, we were sitting in the office of my father's pulmonologist at Robert Wood Johnson University Hospital and listening to a grim diagnosis.

Mechanically, I took notes of the conversation. The disease had already reduced my father's lung capacity by more than 40%. As things worsened, low oxygen levels in his blood would begin to put extra pressure on his heart. Drugs could slow the progress of the disease, but they came with tradeoffs. One was bad for heart patients, like my father. Another had potential side effects that might damage his already weakened lungs.

We all knew the disease would kill him, but the question was when. The doctor said he would try one of the medications to see if it slowed the progress of the disease. There was also physical therapy that might help Dad maximize the use of the lung capacity he still had. If the medication worked, it could prolong his life by a few years.

Driving home to Virginia after that appointment, I began to confront the reality that my father was likely to die, and not in some distant, imagined future, but soon. Perhaps very soon. Before any of his grandchildren finished college, got married or gave him great-grandchildren.

I had always known in a vague, general sense, that my father was the model against which I judged myself and other people. But now, forced to confront the inevitability of losing him, I began thinking harder about what that actually meant.

Dad had never been one for prescriptive parenting. There was no list of rules he taught me and my siblings to obey in order to be good people and productive members of society. He never set specific targets for us to hit in terms of education, career goals, or wealth. His expectations were much more general in nature, and they were articulated more by example than by instruction.

As a child, I didn't understand what my father did for a living, but I knew he worked hard at it. For years, he was out of the house every morning before I woke up, leaving a faint aroma of coffee and aftershave in the kitchen, and he didn't make it home until after — sometimes well after — 7 p.m. Often I'd find him sitting in the living room in the evenings, still working after dinner.

He never complained about working long hours or about his commute to and from Manhattan. From that, I internalized that working hard is simply what a person does — or ought to do.

I never saw my father intentionally disrespect anyone or tolerate being disrespected himself. He never told me that I ought to treat people with dignity and expect the same in return, but because that's what I saw him do, I came to understand that it was what I should do.

Before his retirement and even more so afterward, he dedicated an enormous amount of time to service. He ran youth basketball programs, took leadership roles at his church, served on boards and worked with at-risk youth. He spent countless hours volunteering as a photographer at charity events. He never told me that it was my responsibility to try to be of service to other people. But because it's what he did, I came to see it as expected.

My father wasn't one for mottos or mantras. But it occurred to me that "Do the right thing" might have suited him.

———————

As the coronavirus pandemic spread and the country slowly shut down in the spring of 2020, I tried to focus on writing the book. I began working my way through it, sending a new chapter to Cathy and John Pepper every few weeks and getting positive feedback.

But even as I meticulously detailed Smale's years as CEO, I kept hearing Ed Artzt telling me that I didn't have the man.

I worked through the doubts, intent on meeting a self-imposed goal of a draft completed by the summertime.

Meanwhile, COVID-19 was ravaging New York and New Jersey that spring, sending my parents into isolation.

The medicine wasn't working, and Dad's lungs were getting worse. Nobody said it out loud, but if he caught the virus, no one doubted that he'd be dead in a matter of weeks.

The hospitals in New Jersey were so overwhelmed that it was difficult for Dad to schedule appointments to monitor his condition. The physical-therapy sessions to improve his breathing were canceled.

In July, after months of being locked down at home, my wife and I decided to take our family up to the Adirondacks for a break. On the way, we stopped in New Jersey and had a "socially distant" outdoor dinner at my sister's home. In the car, I had a big box from Kinko's holding two copies of the first draft of this book — one for each parent to read. I'd written everything but the final chapter.

It had been two months since I had last seen my father. Despite warnings from my sisters, I wasn't prepared for what I saw when he made his way from the car and into the back yard.

He was, by this point, practically skeletal. The light-colored polo shirt he wore hung like a ship's sail on a windless day. His arms had shed almost all of their muscle and seemed lost inside his sleeves.

He had bought a portable oxygen concentrator — a self-contained, light-weight alternative to an oxygen tank — and he had it hanging from a strap over his shoulder, the long plastic tubing attached to a cannula that sat just below his nose.

The only thing that hadn't changed was his smile. In pictures I took that evening, his smile looks like it always had, big, broad and easy, as he sits with my mother, raising a glass of wine in a toast to something I can't even remember.

At the end of the evening, I transferred the two manuscript copies into my parents' car. I hadn't been able to shake the feeling that something was missing from the book I'd now nearly finished writing. For that reason, it bothered me to show it to my parents. But I needed a break from writing, and I figured two fresh sets of eyes would be a good thing.

The next morning, my wife and I headed up to Lake Placid with the kids.

————

Through most of that summer, my father had been able to continue taking walks with my mother. They didn't move quickly, but they would cover some ground, going a mile or two before heading home. One evening, though, Mom told me that Dad had been unable to make it more than a few hundred yards from the house.

The hope was that this was a temporary setback, but it wasn't. Eventually, we would learn that his left lung had partially collapsed. Reinflating it was riskier than leaving it alone, and, at 77, Dad was not a candidate for a lung transplant.

I called Dad when I found out, not knowing exactly what I was going to say. We had all thought, at first, that he had at least a few years left. But now, even though no doctor had officially said so, we were all wondering whether it was really just months.

I asked him if there was anything he wanted or needed to do. I asked him if he wanted to see the Adirondacks one last time. We would find a way to make it happen if he did.

No, he told me. He didn't want to take any trips. "I'm in a good place," he said.

In mid-August, on the advice of his pulmonologist, my father went to the University of Pennsylvania Medical Center in Philadelphia for an evaluation. Friends drove my parents to the hospital, and Mom and Dad spent the best part of two days stuck in the emergency room because the regular rooms were all full of COVID-19 patients. When he was finally examined by a doctor, all he got was confirmation of what he had already been told.

Just seven months after his diagnosis, and weeks before his 78th birthday, Dad came home from the hospital, hungry and exhausted. He had decided to enter hospice care. There would be no further treatment of his disease. Medical care would be limited to keeping him comfortable and maximizing the quality of what remained of his life.

I was in New Jersey at the time and was with him that night. I snapped a picture of him not long after he got home. In it, he's sitting up on the sofa, surrounded by plates full of cheese and crackers, fruit and raw vegetables — a pre-dinner "nosh," as my parents called it. In his left hand, he's holding a glass of red wine. At the hospital, he'd made a point of getting the doctor to say — in front of my mother — that it would be all right for him to have a little wine in the evening. He is smiling as though nothing were wrong, just looking glad to be home.

———

By the time Dad began hospice care, I still hadn't written the concluding chapter of the book. I tried several times, but standing in my way was this persistent feeling that, for all the details I had captured, all the stories I had heard and retold, I still hadn't really captured the essence of John Smale.

It also didn't help that, at the same time that I was trying to sum up the life of a man I had never met, I was watching my father's life come to an end.

Sometime around September, I finally gave up. I wouldn't be finishing the book in the foreseeable future.

CHAPTER 9

An Unexpected Discovery

John Smale's habit of saving things made writing about his life much easier than it might have otherwise been. Scrapbooks filled with old letters and photographs told the story of his time at P&G and General Motors and gave me a lot of insight into his history, his thinking, and his relationships with other people.

My father, too, kept things. And in the final months of his life, the project that consumed him more than any other was organizing his files and records so that my mother wouldn't be left to sift through thousands of documents.

I spent days bringing folder after folder to him on the sofa where he now spent his time, permanently connected to an oxygen machine. When the three piles of papers on the floor — file, recycle, and shred — got high enough, I'd dispose of one load and bring more folders for him to go through.

Sometimes, when he dozed off, I worked my way through old letters on company letterhead, congratulating him on a recent promotion, praising his performance in a new position or just explaining what new benefits were available to him as he climbed his way up the corporate ladder.

Dad had joined the Manufacturers Hanover Trust Co. in the 1960s, when it was one of the biggest banks in New York. Its roots dated to Hanover Bank, which was founded in 1851, just 14 years after Procter & Gamble.

As a boy, I had the sense that my father was proud of the organization he worked for. I remember doing my math homework with the black and silver Manufacturers Hanover Trust pencils that he carried in his briefcase. Before I could name the president of the United States, I knew that the bank's president was John McGillicuddy, much, I suspect, as the children of P&G employees in the 1980s knew the name of John Smale. On the rare occasion when I got to visit my father at work, I was always awed by the soaring marble walls and giant brass doors of the hundred-year-old bank buildings.

Manufacturers Hanover Trust had a reputation for steadiness and reliability, and my father mirrored that both in behavior and appearance. I once heard one of his colleagues joke that my father's only concession to "casual Friday" was a blue button-down shirt under his suit jacket, rather than a white one. In the city, the shorthand name for the bank was "Manny Hanny," but I never heard my father refer to it by anything other than its full name or, occasionally, "MHT."

I was finishing college by the time a cycle of financial mergers caught up with MHT. In 1991, the company merged with Chemical Bank. I was genuinely surprised at how angry I felt when my father told me that the combined institutions would use the Chemical name and that Manufacturers Hanover Trust would effectively cease to exist.

My father survived the merger, unlike many of his colleagues, and found himself comfortable in Chemical's corporate culture. But a few years later, Chemical merged with Chase Manhattan; a few years after that, the bank merged again, this time with J.P. Morgan. He survived those mergers, too, but with each one, I could sense his personal connection to the institution, and its shifting corporate culture, growing more and more tenuous.

Before the series of mergers began to eat away at the bank's character, I imagine my father thought about Manufacturers Hanover Trust the way John Smale felt about P&G.

Smale once described good companies as those that "represent a character. They have an ethos to them. They perpetuate themselves, if they're really well-grounded in their character. They do well, I think, primarily because they have as a foundation a character that allows people — encourages people, really — to dedicate a working life to them."

My father had dedicated the greater part of a working life to Manufacturers Hanover Trust, and I can only imagine that, at the time, he expected to retire from the bank one day and watch it move on as a going concern, the way thousands of P&G alums do.

But that wasn't to be. Today, virtually nothing in my parents' home would tell you what my father did for a living.

The only thing that offers a clue is part of a china place setting that sits, oddly out of place, on a bookshelf in the family room. From a distance, the dinner plate, coffee cup and saucer are understated and unremarkable. But on closer inspection you can see, in subtle gold leaf, the Manufacturers Hanover Trust logo. The remnants from the old executive dining room had been gifts to my father from other former MHT employees.

Dad treasured them in a way I never really understood until I began this book.

One afternoon, I was trying to make sense of a decades-old life insurance policy when my father suddenly sat up in surprise. He had a folder full of papers in his hand, and he silently held one out to me with a look of something between amusement and amazement.

It was a memo on Paul Fitzgerald's JP Morgan Private Bank stationery with information about an upcoming fishing trip to the Cascapédia. The memo had multiple addressees, in addition to my father. There was Chauncey Loomis, the author and historian, and William F. Pounds, the dean of the MIT Sloan School of Management.

I blinked when I saw the next entry: "John G. Smale (Chris Caldemeyer)."

Apparently, my father had forgotten that, in August 2003, he had gone fishing with John Smale.

I was dumbstruck. Dad had told me about his trips with Paul Fitzgerald and about many of the people he met on them. There were corporate titans with egos as large as their salaries, and scions of the generationally wealthy, whose surnames adorned buildings and were attached to endowed chairs at major universities.

The reporter in me wanted to pump him for information, but it was clear to both of us that he really didn't have any.

As he looked back on the trip, though, Dad realized that he hadn't recognized who Smale was. His only memory of him was that he must have been "that nice guy who was there with his grandson."

It occurred to me that Smale would probably have been pleased by the description.

———————

In early September, a hospice nurse took my mother aside and told her to prepare for the possibility of a sudden decline in my father's health. Hearing that news, I knew I could no longer postpone something I had been thinking about for months: I needed to tell my father what he meant to me.

I am not normally a very emotional person, but I did choke back tears telling him not just that I loved him but that I also respected him. That when I had a decision to make, I asked myself what he would do. That he was my role model, my standard for what a person ought to be.

He had kind words for me. He told me he loved me and was proud of me. He talked about me, my wife and my two sons and stepdaughter, and how much he enjoyed their company. He talked about the book. He had read and commented on the early chapters, but over time the medication had made it hard for him to focus for long stretches of time.

He continued, and his tone changed slightly. He told me that, since it had become evident that he was dying, he had been deluged by calls and notes from grateful people whose lives he had touched in one way or another. The thanks and praise were troubling him.

"It's like they're talking about someone else," he said. "I know myself, and I know I'm not the person they're describing."

"Dad," I said, "they're describing you as they experienced you. And that experience was real. What you think about it doesn't change the impact you had on them."

We spoke a little while longer. Until there was nothing else to say. We agreed on that specifically, each of us promising the other that there was nothing between us that had been left unsaid.

I didn't realize it at the time, but that last gift he gave me — certainty about how he thought of me as a son and as a man, and acceptance of how much I loved and respected him — would make the difficult months to come bearable and, unexpectedly, beautiful.

———

My father died about 20 minutes before midnight on Dec. 19, 2020, surrounded by my mother, my parents' four children, and my brother-in-law. It hadn't even been a year since his diagnosis of pulmonary fibrosis. The months leading up to his death were hard. In his final weeks, my mother, brother, sisters and I cycled through the seat at his bedside as his ability to manage day-to-day tasks diminished, then eventually disappeared.

My father's care was enabled by every member of the family, including my siblings, our spouses, and our children. My father's closest friend from childhood and his wife made frequent trips to New Jersey from upstate New York, as did my father's sister and her youngest son.

Because of the pandemic, we could not hold any of the typical services that help the living place the dead in the context of memory. The countless small tales told at wakes and funerals, some previously unknown to even the deceased's closest relatives, weren't available to us.

We had a small, socially distanced funeral Mass in my parents' church. My mother's florist had prepared an inspired arrangement for the casket, with greenery and flowers intertwined with fishing gear.

Then, we all went home, to start living life again.

———————

My father's care had pulled my attention away from day-to-day work on the book, and it was difficult to bring myself back to it. I suppose part of the problem was the mental tension inherent in describing one man's legacy as I was trying to understand my own father's.

But there was more to it than that. It was becoming clear to me that, in a very serious way, I had failed Cathy.

When I first met her and listened to her talk about her hopes for a book about her dad, I approached the task with a reporter's typical detachment. I understood at some level that this was deeply important to her, of course, but I wasn't emotionally invested in the project. In fact, every instinct I had pushed me away from emotional investment. It made for bad reporting and created giant analytical blind spots.

The John Smale book was a job — one I would do to the best of my ability — but still, just a job.

Now, though, that approach felt utterly insufficient to the task that had been set before me, to the trust that had been placed in my hands.

I understood now, in a way I hadn't a year before, that Cathy had wanted a memorial to her father — the same sort of treatment I would want for my father. I had delivered what amounted to a book-length newspaper article about John Smale's business career.

Now, every time I opened the "Smale" folder on my computer, I felt utterly overwhelmed. I had no idea how to turn the book I had already written into the book I should have written.

CHAPTER 10

A Way Forward

One day in 2021, when I ought to have been working on the book, I started thinking about all the messages Dad told me he had received from people when they learned that he had gone into hospice care.

I was the executor of his estate, and I had made sure that I had access to his email accounts. So I logged in and began scrolling backwards.

The deluge had begun a week after his last trip to the hospital. He had sent a brief note to a group of old friends, colleagues and acquaintances explaining his situation. That note had been forwarded out to many, many more people, and within hours the responses had started to pour in.

I started reading through them. Amid the exclamations of dismay and sadness, there were stories.

A man in his early 70s had grown up in the same neighborhood as my father, and he wrote about a small act of kindness Dad had shown him when they were children. It was 65 years in the past, but it still stuck in his memory.

There were stories about fishing trips, road trips and vacations.

"You are my friend of over 60 years. We were brothers in high school," one read. "We roamed the Adirondacks from Inlet to Bolton Landing. ... We were comrades in the service of our country."

A woman who had worked for my father decades before told him that, having lost her own parents at a young age, she had looked to him as a surrogate father as she tried to navigate her way through work and life. "Your steadiness, your integrity, your grace, your great smile and your encouragement in the face of challenge remain things on which I look back and realize just how important they were to my growth and stability."

A friend of my brother wrote to say he had always seen my father as a role model.

Another woman who worked for my father wrote, "If there's a silver lining in this, it's that I have the opportunity to tell you what a positive impact working with you had on me, even now, more than 18 years later. You led by example, never allowing ego or seniority to influence a decision and showed me that kindness and empathy were the best solution to any situation."

I saw from the timestamps that the notes had poured in over the course of several days in a staggering tidal wave of emotion. I could understand how Dad had found it overwhelming.

One thing I noticed was that a stranger could have read through all of those messages and tributes and come away with virtually no idea of what my father had done for a living.

The people who had known him the longest had loved him before he ever thought about becoming a banker. The people who had come to know him after his retirement probably had only a vague understanding of what he had done in his working life.

But crucially, even in the notes from people who had worked closely with him, some for years, there was nothing about the things Dad had achieved in his career. No mention of big decisions made, major clients landed or profit targets reached.

Everything people remembered about my father was about how he had treated them, what they had learned from watching him, and how his example had changed them, not as bankers, but as people.

In boxes and albums in my office, I have copies of some of the letters and emails John Smale received after his own diagnosis with pulmonary fibrosis. I had originally paid them scant attention. My focus was on Smale's time running P&G and General Motors, not the end of his life.

But upon rereading them, it was impossible not to hear echoes of the notes sent to my father. Nobody had written to a dying John Smale to remind him of big acquisitions, successful product rollouts or corporate restructurings. Business associates and friends reached out when they learned Smale's condition was terminal so that they could thank him for the role he had played in their lives.

"You have made a difference in my life, John," one woman wrote. "I was one of those watching you work at P&G, seeing how you not only managed the business but those around you. You will never know the absolute reach of your mentoring and coaching — but I can tell you this — your legacy lives on in those who have emulated you over the years."

"The reason I'm writing this is to tell you how much your kindness has meant to me over the years," another woman wrote.

I found a note from John Pepper, who was serving as chairman of the board of the Walt Disney Corp. at the time. "I trust you know how much you live as a role model for me to this very day. When I am thinking of what I should do ... I ask myself what might you do. Of all the great leaders I have known, you are the finest."

Some are more personal.

"You probably know this, but your legacy is something that we all strive for," wrote Lisa Diedrichs, Cathy's daughter and Smale's oldest grandchild. "I hope you can look back at your life and smile in satisfaction. You deserve it. You are an icon for me, and always will be."

Seventeen at the time, Cathy's youngest child, Madeline Caldemeyer, wrote, "The whole world knows what a success you were professionally, but what only our family and friends know is what a success you were personally as well. You have been the best role model to me for the past seventeen years, and I want you to know that both you and Grandma will influence me in school, work, as well as relationships, for the rest of my life."

————————

Over the next few days, I began going back through the thousands of pages of interview transcripts I had compiled. I had mined them for details already. I had pulled out names and dates and recollections about who was in the room when key decisions were made. But I had left behind so much more.

Again and again, as I worked my way through those pages, I came to spots where people I was interviewing broke away from the question I wanted them to answer so they could tell me about a brief interaction with Smale that had changed the way they thought about themselves or about their job.

I found descriptions of elaborate practical jokes Smale had played on friends, and times when he had delivered words of comfort or consolation at just the right moment. There were stories about his generosity, his dedication, and above all, of his abiding love for his wife, Phyllis.

Ed Artzt had been mostly right. It wasn't that I didn't have the man, not exactly. It was that I had the man, but I had left half of him out of the book.

Finally, I was beginning to see a way forward. I needed to stop telling the story of John Smale from the perspective of a reporter, and instead let the people who loved him explain what he had meant to them.

John Smale and sister Joy as young children

John Smale and Phyllis Weaver at a Miami University college dance

John and Phyllis Smale on their wedding day at the Weaver family home in Evansville, Indiana

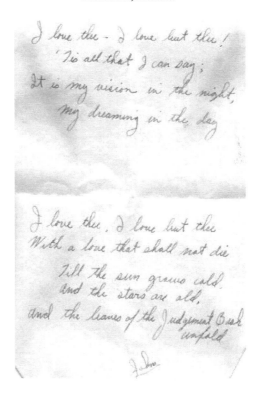

A romantic Valentine's Day poem written by John Smale for Phyllis while in college

John and Phyllis Smale dancing at a family wedding, 1977

The Smale family goofing around

The Smale family following John Smale's promotion to P&G President, 1974

Extended Smale family Christmas celebration, 1982

John and Phyllis Smale in front of Egyptian pyramids during P&G business trip

John Smale salmon fishing in Canada

John Smale with record-setting tarpon, caught while fly-fishing in Marathon, Florida

*Geese sculpture commissioned by Smale children in honor of John and Phyllis Smale's
50th Wedding Anniversary (Credit: Hannah Breidinger Tishey)*

Richard R. Deupree, President and Chairman of the Board, P&G, 1930-1959

Ed Harness, Chairman and CEO, P&G, 1974-1981

Crest toothpaste advertising after earning
American Dental Association endorsement, 1965

John Smale as a young businessman at the beginning of his P&G career

John Smale in his office shortly after being elected P&G CEO

John Smale in his office as CEO on a typical Saturday

John Smale with fellow P&G executives Tom Laco, John Pepper and Ed Artzt, 1986

John Smale with fellow retired P&G executives Wolfgang Berndt, Gordon Brunner and Jerry Dirvin, 2009

John Smale greeting Chinese premier Deng Xiaoping during Time-Life tour of US business leaders following China's opening to the West, 1985 (Credit: P&G)

John Smale "passing the torch" to newly elected P&G CEO Ed Artzt, 1989

"Each individual can make a real difference."

John G. Smale

*"No factor has played a more important role in the success
of R&D at P&G than its record of hiring and retaining some
of the most talented people in the industry."*

John G. Smale

The John G. Smale Innovation Award is designed to recognize the spirit of innovative
thinking that leads to significant scientific or technological advancements. The winners
of this award indeed have a right to be proud, for they are the future of our Company.

*John G. Smale Innovation Award plaque, presented to outstanding P&G R&D
innovation leaders each year*

*(Left-Right): John F. (Jack) Smith, Louis R. Hughes, George R. (Rick) Wagoner, Michael
Porter, (professor of strategy at Harvard Business School), and John G. Smale during GM
"Overseas Recognition Dinner," 1996 (Credit: General Motors)*

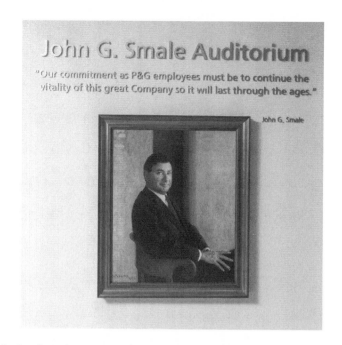

John Smale Auditorium at P&G Corporate Headquarters, dedicated in 2010
(Credit: Ross Van Pelt)

John Smale teaching young grandson Chris Caldemeyer to fish, at a lake in Michigan

PART THREE

CHAPTER 11

Taking the Long View

In one of one of my sessions with Ed Artzt, he said that Smale had a way of looking to the future that most of his colleagues did not. Once I set out to retell part of John Smale's story through the eyes of the people who had known and loved him, I noticed that many others had made the same observation. It came up again and again, in interview after interview.

Peg Wyant, the first female executive to come up through the ranks at P&G, told me about a meeting with Smale in 1978, when he was president. With three children at home and a husband who was running an entirely different company, Wyant was looking to pare back her responsibilities at P&G. But her boss called her into his office one day and said that Smale wanted her to come work for him.

"I felt I needed to go work with the president like I needed a hole in the head," she told me. She declined two different offers passed down through her superiors. Then she was asked to meet Smale in his office.

When she sat down in the president's office on the 11th floor, she told me, Smale got right to the point: "I'm looking for someone to help me figure out what Procter & Gamble should be in the next millennium."

"And that really did hit me," she told me. "I thought, I don't know of many people on this earth who think in those terms. ... The next millennium was more than 20 years away."

Smale wanted her to identify opportunities for the kind of growth that he knew P&G would need to attract and retain top people in the next century — people who, in 1978, hadn't even been born.

Wyant wound up working on a project that surveyed consumer goods across virtually every product line found in a grocery store. She helped identify several new lines of business that P&G, under Smale's leadership, would enter successfully in the years to come.

But Smale's vision of P&G in the new millennium wasn't restricted to new lines of business. Time after time, Smale made decisions that were designed to make sure the company remained competitive — and continued to grow — for years into the future.

One of the best summations of Smale's ability to take the long view came from George Gibson, who had been the treasurer of P&G for part of Smale's tenure. He described to me a complex set of financial maneuvers he had taken at Smale's urging to move a significant percentage of P&G common stock into the hands of its employees and retirees. The object, he said, was to protect the company from the kind of hostile takeovers that were common in the 1980s.

I asked Gibson, what would have been so awful about a takeover? Flippantly, I added, the worst-case scenario was that Smale walked away with a big payoff and went fishing.

Gibson seemed almost offended by the question. "It's an old company, though, Rob. It's 175 years old, and he didn't want it to end. And if we had a hostile takeover, that would have been the end of Procter & Gamble. We would have been called something else."

Gibson was animated now, as though he really wanted me to understand something important.

"John's idea was, 'We're here forever,'" he said, leaning toward me. "Now, we constantly improve and so forth and so on. But we're here forever."

I had to sit with that for a while before I really understood it. The assumption that "we're here forever" explained a lot about the way Smale thought about the company and the way he made decisions. People praise executives for being able to "see around corners," but Smale had been operating on an entirely different scale.

I began paging back through my notes and the original draft of the book, looking at some of Smale's key decisions from a new angle.

———————

In 1980, the year before Smale was promoted to CEO, Artzt was put in charge of almost all of P&G's international business. Not long afterward, at the same time that Smale's promotion to CEO was announced, Artzt was given the final piece of P&G's international operation, a business in Japan that had been bleeding money for nearly a decade.

Smale's elevation to CEO would change their working relationship in a significant way. As president of the company, Smale had not had responsibility for its international operations, so their paths hadn't crossed very frequently.

Since he would now be reporting directly to Smale, Artzt figured it would be a good idea to sit down with his new boss and set some expectations.

"John," Artzt said, "let's see if we can't agree on a strategy for the business for the next few years. I want to make sure that we get a mutual understanding of what we're trying to do, so that we're not fighting in the trenches over each proposal."

Smale replied immediately. "It's very simple, Ed. We're a company that supplies products to men and women all over the world. We've been far too slow in getting them out there. I want you to take us global."

It was a command Artzt had been waiting to hear for years. He had spent part of the previous decade revitalizing the company's operations in Europe. Now, Smale was handing Artzt a mandate to expand P&G's presence overseas, everywhere it was feasible to do so. There was an unspoken urgency to the effort. P&G had been slow to expand internationally and couldn't wait any longer.

"John, it's going to be expensive. We're going to need people. But we can do it," Artzt said. "If you want to go global, goddammit, we'll go global."

Smale looked across his desk and nodded. Artzt reached out and shook Smale's hand.

"We'll get you the rest of the world," he promised.

————————

One serious obstacle stood in the way of getting the rest of the world, and that was Japan.

P&G had struggled since 1972 to find success there and had nothing to show for it but annual losses in the tens of millions of dollars and an increasingly frustrated board of directors.

"The Company's entire entry strategy was wrong and had to be changed," Artzt told me. "P&G had chosen to treat Japan like an export market, where products and marketing strategies that had been successful in the U.S. were deployed virtually intact." The premise was that what had worked for P&G in the United States should work elsewhere, including Japan.

"Unfortunately, Japan was quite different," Artzt continued. "It had highly innovative entrenched local competitors in every one of P&G's major business categories. Moreover, the habits and practices of Japanese consumers were different enough to require tailoring of our products, and P&G had not done that as part of its entry strategy.

"As a result, our products were deficient, and our advertising and marketing strategies tended to be irrelevant or insensitive to Japanese culture or consumer experience," Artzt said.

When Smale took over as CEO, the board informed him in no uncertain terms that the company had one more bite at the apple in Japan, and then it would be time to cut P&G's losses and move on.

In early 1982, Smale made his first trip to Japan, for a meeting with the country management team in Osaka. He'd spent considerable time reviewing the Japanese operation, he told them, noting that "1981 was a difficult year for your business." But he asked them not to be discouraged.

"Perhaps you have noticed that I keep referring to 'your business,'" Smale told them. "This is because this is your business. The Procter & Gamble Company can provide help to make the Japanese business successful, but the company cannot create that success. The Japanese business will succeed or fail based on the efforts of all of you here today."

When I read the text of Smale's comments, I could sense the frustration he was feeling. In a way, he was having to explain to P&G employees what it really meant to work for P&G.

"You must produce the products with the highest standards of quality at the lowest possible cost," he said. "You must sell these products and see that they are in full retail distribution. You must advertise the benefits of these products to the Japanese consumers in a manner that will encourage consumers to buy them.

"And, to do all this, you must understand the Japanese consumers better than anyone else — any competitor. Their habits and practices. Their likes and dislikes. You must surround the products you make with knowledge of the users of these products."

This was the sort of message that would be drilled into an assistant brand manager in Cincinnati during his first few months on the job. Yet here was the CEO of the company trying to impress the most basic tenets of the company's philosophy on senior managers of a major segment of its international business.

"Procter & Gamble is a proud company," Smale said. "We are the most successful developer, manufacturer and marketer of consumer products throughout the world. Procter & Gamble is also a patient company. Not everything we undertake is an immediate success. We are willing to stick with our plans — to persevere — as long as we remain convinced that our plans are sound and will eventually prove successful."

The message was both an exhortation and a warning. P&G would give these executives the tools they needed to turn the business around, and the time to do it — as long as Smale and the board of directors believed progress was being made.

Left unspoken, though plainly understood, was that, after a decade of costly failure, their patience was dwindling.

As I read through the history of P&G's involvement in Japan, I found it difficult to understand why Smale had been so reluctant to give up on the business there. Surely there were other untapped markets around the world where the resources dedicated to Japan could meet with better results?

It turned out that someone had asked Smale that very question. Durk Jager, who would become the CEO of P&G many years later, had listened to Smale describe the company's struggles in Japan over dinner in 1981.

Smale, Jager told me, said this: "It seems very clear to me, particularly with what's going on with Japanese competitors with automobiles and communications, that if we're not able to compete with the Japanese in Japan, we're in for some problems. Certainly in the Far East, and perhaps around the world."

Once again, Smale had been looking far beyond the immediate problem — the company losing money in Japan — at a much larger issue. A decade later, American companies' fear of being swallowed whole by "Japan, Inc." would be the subject of much handwringing in the business press, and would even bleed over into popular culture, in novels like Michael Crichton's *Rising Sun* and Tom Clancy's *Debt of Honor*. But Smale was focused on the problem as early as 1981.

Two years after that conversation, as the business in Japan continued to stagnate, Smale would make a return visit.

His approach this time was very different. Even Artzt, who knew what was at stake, was surprised at how forceful and blunt the CEO was the second time around.

Addressing a crowd of managers, Smale noted the continued losses in the Japanese business and the lackluster sales growth, and said, "We're not going to put up with this any longer. We either fix this business in the next year, or you're all out of a job, and we're out of Japan."

Artzt later told me that it was the toughest speech he had ever watched Smale give, particularly given the audience: In Japanese business culture at the time, executives who lost their jobs were treated like damaged goods and would face real difficulty finding other employment.

Smale made it clear that Jager, who was now in charge of P&G's operations in Japan, had a mandate from the CEO to overhaul the internal dynamics of the business.

The combination of Jager, a motivated young manager looking to make a name for himself, and a workforce motivated by the prospect of losing their livelihoods turned out to be exactly what P&G needed. Over the next year, Artzt and Jager made key leadership changes in Japan. American expatriates were moved out, and Japanese employees received more responsibility. The next step was launching a program called *Ichidai Hiyaku*, which Jager translated as "The Great Flying Leap."

Jager had the Japanese management team rededicate itself to P&G's commitment to knowing the customer and producing the products they wanted. Diapers were overhauled, producing a version of Pampers that was so well suited to the Japanese market that, within five years, it would command the highest market share of any disposable diaper in Japan.

Still struggling in the laundry detergent space, P&G introduced a new "compact" detergent, Ariel. Jager also began looking to broaden the number of categories where P&G could compete.

The biggest success among the new entries would be Whisper, feminine-hygiene pads that relied on P&G's newest technology. Whisper pads, sized specifically for Japanese women, were an immediate success, surging to the top share in the market, even while selling at a 24% premium to the competition.

Soon enough, it was clear that the turnaround had begun. Between 1985 and 1988, P&G's annual sales in Japan would more than triple to $566 million, validating the time, effort, and investment that Smale and two CEOs before him had poured into the country.

"We were in an investment phase until 1986, 13 years after we had entered Japan," Smale would reflect in 1989. "Last year we made a good profit in Japan. This year we will make a better profit. We now have major products in 13 different product categories in Japan. We believe that in the years ahead, it's possible that Japan could become our largest and most profitable international subsidiary. Companies like Procter & Gamble must, I believe, have managers who are free to make investment decisions that are going to cover multi-year periods and have boards which are willing to back those decisions."

———————

During the mid-1980s, Smale would make what was arguably the most important decision of his tenure as CEO, acquiring Richardson-Vicks International. This was the deal John Pepper had remembered so vividly in our first meeting, when Smale made the snap decision to raise P&G's offer to outbid a rival.

But what hadn't been clear to me at the time was that Smale had been laying the groundwork for the deal for a decade before it happened.

Smale had been in occasional contact with the leadership of RVI — the corporate descendant of the Vick Chemical Co., which had hired him out of college. RVI had leading brands in a number of attractive consumer-products markets. Equally important, it had a major overseas presence in markets where P&G had struggled.

More than once, Smale had floated the possibility of a merger, with little success. Then, in 1985, P&G's archrival, Unilever, mounted a hostile-takeover effort. Inside the Richardson-Vicks boardroom, this move was met with horror. Setting aside the difficulty of unwillingly merging two established companies, the board members didn't believe that RVI's corporate culture was compatible with Unilever's.

The RVI board began looking for a "white knight" to acquire the company. Because Smale had been prescient enough to plant a seed ahead of time, P&G was the natural choice.

Geoff Boisi, who was running the investment bank at Goldman Sachs at the time, advised P&G on the deal. He told me that, in a decade advising P&G, he had come to see Smale as "the quintessential business statesman" and said that the Richardson-Vicks deal was nothing short of "courageous."

The billion-dollar deal was the largest acquisition in P&G's history, and it had faced real internal resistance, with many senior executives in Cincinnati believing that Smale was overpaying.

Boisi had been on the other end of the phone line when Smale made the decision to add a dollar per share to P&G's bid.

"There were strongly held feelings among different people, but because of the relationship of trust that we developed with John, he took our advice, and I think that dollar did make a difference," Boisi said. "It was a decisive move and a courageous move, and I think it worked out really well for Procter & Gamble."

That, of course, was an understatement. The deal with Richardson-Vicks brought in major new products, including Oil of Olay, Pantene and the company's well-known line of cough and cold remedies. It also gave P&G a much-needed foothold in multiple countries, enabling the company to introduce its products to billions of new consumers.

It was, again, another example of Smale looking much further ahead than most of the executives in the room when the time for a key decision arrived.

"He had this marvelous, intuitive, in-the-blood feeling of growth," John Pepper told me, while talking about the RVI deal. "He was looking at what we were going to do in the next generation."

―――――――

The fight to succeed in Japan and the Richardson-Vicks acquisition were not the only milestones in P&G's global expansion in the 1980s.

In 1985, Jorge Montoya was in the tricky position of trying to manage P&G's nascent Latin American operations from Cincinnati. A native of Peru, Montoya had joined the company in 1971, after graduating from the University of California at Berkeley, and had worked his way up through the organization.

At the time, P&G's Latin America division consisted of four markets, Mexico, Puerto Rico, Peru, and Venezuela.

P&G had faced many difficulties and setbacks in its operations south of the U.S. border. Mexico was, by that time, a reasonably mature market, but it had only become so after years of struggle, as different governments continually changed the rules under which foreign companies were allowed to operate. The board of directors was nervous about making a large investment in other countries in the region, but Smale convinced them to take a chance on Montoya's team.

Montoya was convinced that P&G wouldn't really succeed in Latin America unless it made a tangible commitment to the market, including a commitment of senior-level leadership. Smale approved, and by 1987, Montoya had moved the leadership team for Latin America to Caracas. Before he left, Smale reminded him about the board's concerns, and said it would be up to Montoya to convince them that the investment was a good one.

"Make money, convince the company that it is worth investing, then we'll help you invest," Smale said.

By 1988, P&G's Latin American operations were running a modest profit. Price controls in some markets took a bite out of the earnings from other regions, but on balance, the numbers were moving in the right direction.

Pressed by Smale, the board relented and began approving the kind of investment that Montoya would need to make P&G a presence across the entire region, with money for strategic acquisitions, product development, and extensive advertising.

Not long afterward, Smale visited the management team in its new home in Caracas.

"You guys are going to have to build yourself a place where you can have your headquarters," Smale said.

Montoya told me he was stunned. He was still operating on an almost day-to-day basis, focused on making sure that the board didn't lose confidence in the growing operations in Latin America.

"You don't have to do it now, but you ought to have that in mind," Smale continued. "The only thing I would suggest is that when you do, make it so that it's a landmark in the city — a landmark for the region."

Noting the surprise on Montoya's face, he continued, "You need this for the future of this company. We're thinking about 50 years from now, 100 years from now."

Within a few years, in fact, P&G would break ground on a headquarters building in Caracas that was so iconic that generations of residents would grow up using it as a key landmark when giving directions within the city.

———

In addition to its expansion in Latin America in the late 1980s, P&G also moved into the countries of the former Soviet Union. Smale gave the greenlight to the foray into Eastern Europe at the urging of Wolfgang Berndt, a P&G executive who had been born during the Second World War in the German-speaking part of what was then Czechoslovakia.

Berndt had grown up with an interest in and connection to the countries that disappeared behind the Iron Curtain at the end of the war, and in late 1987, he approached Smale with a copy of the book *Perestroika*, by Mikhail Gorbachev, the General Secretary of the Communist Party of the Soviet Union. The book had sent shockwaves through the global political and diplomatic worlds, because in it, Gorbachev sketched out a new vision for the Soviet Union that would throw off years of self-imposed isolation in favor of broader economic ties with the rest of the world.

"John, I think things will change in the East in the not-too-distant future," Berndt said. "And I think it is time for us to start exploring the option of an entry once the conditions change."

P&G had historically been late getting into overseas markets, he reminded Smale, giving its competitors head starts of years or even decades.

"Here we have an opportunity to be, for once, not late," Berndt argued.

Berndt told me that it took Smale all of two weeks to make the decision, in consultation with Ed Artzt, to aggressively push P&G into the markets of the former Soviet republics.

Within a year, P&G would begin moving into Russia, Poland, the Czech Republic, and Hungary, laying the groundwork for a further expansion into the remainder of the region in the following years.

CHAPTER 12

Restructuring for the Future

With Procter & Gamble's international footprint growing ever larger, there was a sense in Cincinnati that the company needed to take affirmative steps to be certain that P&G's corporate culture would persist across oceans and borders.

John Pepper, who was president of the company at the time, told me he was especially concerned about bringing the P&G ethos to these new, far-flung countries, and he approached Smale with the idea of codifying the principles and values of the company in a definitive statement.

At first, Smale was cautious, and Pepper understood why. Pepper had, he admitted, a tendency to take big ideas and run with them, and sometimes Smale saw it as his job to reel things in and make sure they were fulfilling a business purpose.

"Wait a minute," he said, as Pepper pitched the idea. "What is this, really? What are we trying to do? Is this really important?"

I think I understand why he initially hesitated. To Smale and other P&G leaders of his generation, the principles of the company did not need to be written down. Rather, they were passed on by example, day in and day out.

It was the daily lunches Smale had attended as a young executive, with current and past leaders of the company assembled around the table, that had been the wellspring of the company's values, not some written statement.

Smale believed that a company's character was created over generations by the people who led it. In an interview, he once explained how he had seen the company's values passed from R.R. Deupree to Neil McElroy, who ran P&G from 1948 to 1957 before leaving to become secretary of defense. They continued through Howard Morgens, who ran P&G until 1974, and on to Ed Harness, Smale's close friend, who preceded him in the CEO's office.

Smale traced many of the principles back to the company's founders, who had sensed that the market value of a reputation for providing goods "at full weight and correct tare" and the business value of developing a workforce with its well-being tied to the well-being of the company itself.

"They're all aspects of the company's character — it's really words that are backed up by actions. Because all of this really was well-entrenched long before we had anything on paper in the way of statement of principles or character or anything like that," Smale had said.

But Pepper was persistent, and Smale had the foresight to understand that, as the company grew, it simply wasn't practical to expect its values to take hold organically in dozens of countries, some thousands of miles from Cincinnati. Soon, he went from dubious to deeply committed.

Over a period of months — lightning speed for an operation like P&G, which defined its culture in decades — Pepper and Smale worked with dozens of company leaders to put the core truths on paper.

As the project got started, Pepper realized that most of the hard work had already been done by the generations of leaders who had come before. The document that would come to be titled "P&G Purpose, Values & Principles" was not so much prescriptive, he realized, as descriptive.

"We weren't really making anything up," Pepper recalled, telling me about how he and Smale worked through different iterations of the statement. "Basically, what we were doing was reflecting on what was the essence of this place. It wasn't, 'Here's what we hope to be compared to where we are now.' It's a statement of what we are at our best."

The resulting document, known within the company as "PVP," would change little over the coming decades. It served as a reminder to longtime P&G employees of the standards the company expected them to meet, and it was a guide for new hires, telling them what they could expect from the company and what it would expect in return.

The succinct statement of purpose at the beginning demonstrated both the simplicity and the broad scope of what drove Smale throughout his career with the company.

> We will provide branded products and services of superior quality and value that improve the lives of the world's consumers, now and for generations to come. As a result, consumers will reward us with leadership sales, profit and value creation, allowing our people, our shareholders and the communities in which we live and work to prosper.

———————

The adoption of the PVP statement demonstrated Smale's understanding of the importance of preserving essential elements of Procter & Gamble's culture. But he also recognized when it was time to implement dramatic change.

In the middle of Smale's term as CEO, P&G suffered the first year-over-year decline in profits in more than 30 years. Pepper had told me the story, when we first met, of how Smale had rejected a proposal to withhold marketing support for three crucial new products in order to pad the profit figures and save him the embarrassment.

In a letter to a colleague that summer, Smale wrote, "It's funny. Part of me — the great majority — hasn't really been bothered by our profit performance (and the attending press articles) of the last year because I am convinced that what we are doing is essential for the long-term future of the Company and because I think we will succeed in what we are doing. ... Then, of course, there is another part of me. That's the part that wakes up at 3:00 in the morning and thinks about the fact that I am the first head of this business that has gone through a year of down profits since 1952. And that's not much fun."

Procter & Gamble would move on from its lackluster financial performance in 1985 to post much stronger numbers in 1986, but the experience left Smale with lingering concerns about company operations.

There had been no indication at the beginning of 1985, as divisions made their forecasts for the year, that profits would drop from the year before. But as Smale received monthly updates, he saw that, in instance after instance, results were slipping further away from the projections.

Even as profits began to revive the following year, Smale was unsatisfied. A system that delivered a 1985-style shock once could do it again. Therefore, the system needed to change.

Smale was also unhappy with the company's performance in one particular area. P&G was a very profitable company, but by one of the metrics it most strongly associated with success — market share — it was struggling. In every fiscal year since 1979, more P&G brands lost market share than gained market share. In aggregate, the company's share in all established brand categories had slipped from 33% to 31%.

Smale saw the faulty profit forecasting and market share deterioration as related problems. He believed that the key decision-makers at P&G had become too far removed from the consumer to understand what was really necessary to grow brands profitably.

With the acquisition of Richardson-Vicks, P&G now had 39 different product categories, scattered across seven divisions. Several of those divisions were, by themselves, larger than the entire company had been when the division system was created 30 years before.

Sitting above the division structure was another layer of decision-making authority: P&G's "Administrative Committee." A 40-person group of division heads and senior staff executives, it met every week to review and approve many of the operational decisions made within the divisions. It could be extremely frustrating to brand managers, who sometimes needed the committee's sign-off for things as basic as package design modifications.

In this top-heavy management structure, key decisions about the marketing and sales of individual products were made by people or committees far removed from the consumer.

"The thing had really kind of gotten out of hand," Smale later observed. "It no longer had the efficiency and the focus that it once had, as a result of size and complexity."

"We had to refocus the business," he said. "Businesses run best when you have a relatively small, autonomous group of people who are responsible for managing that business, and they are focused."

Working closely with Pepper, Smale began developing what would eventually become the biggest internal restructuring of Procter & Gamble in a generation.

In October 1987, at a meeting of company managers, Smale announced a switch to a system he described as "category management." The company would designate 26 "category general managers" to be in charge of specific product areas — such as hair care, laundry detergent, or disposable diapers. Some would have responsibility for more than one small category, but for the most part, the category managers were to focus their attention on one specific facet of P&G's business.

"The category will be the active business unit of the company," Smale told the crowd. "The category general manager will have direct responsibility for profit, volume, share, cash flow, for the total results of the brands in the category. The category team will be responsible for the product, packaging, copy and sales plans to reach their specific business goals. They will be responsible for new brand activity within the category."

The whole point was to push decision-making responsibility down through the ranks of the company until it rested on the team closest to the consumer. To give category managers the ability to meet those responsibilities, each category would have its own advertising, product development, sales and finance departments.

"The category team will be expected to know that business like they know the palms of their hands. To know consumers, to know the market, to know competitors," Smale said.

"The real responsibility for what goes on in the category is going to be with the category general manager and his or her organization. That's going to be where the buck stops. That's going to be where the focus is. That's where I am going to look for the results."

Explaining the move to a reporter sometime later, Smale said, "The creation of these category profit centers was really a continuation of the basic philosophy that small is good — that you bring focus to a specific business when you create a stand-alone operation."

Smale and Pepper disbanded the decades-old Administrative Committee, replacing it with a 20-member executive committee that would limit its involvement to strategic issues and any operational concerns that couldn't be addressed at a lower level.

A final step, meant in part to prevent another surprise like the profit decline in 1985, was the implementation of a Profit Improvement Plan. The program, for the first time, tied a portion of managers' compensation to profitability, rather than just unit sales volume.

"I wanted ... incentives with these groups so that, when they made a profit commitment, they mean what they say. And barring the unforeseen, they fulfill that agreement," Smale later explained. "There's no rocket science about it. It's simply using incentives to motivate people to do things that you want them to do."

———

Not long after the restructuring was announced, Bob Gill got a call to meet with Smale. Gill was among the first people named to the new category general manager position, with responsibility for "salted snacks," which really meant Pringles potato chips.

The brand had been a millstone around the company's neck for more than a decade. Its original success in the early 1970s had convinced the company that it had another blockbuster on its hands, and management poured tens of millions of dollars into building a giant plant in Jackson, Tenn.

But after committing all that capital to the brand, P&G had to watch as its market share began to shrink. The novelty of shaped potato chips wore off, and consumers began to complain that the taste of Pringles didn't match that of traditional potato chips. When the Food and Drug Administration, under pressure from traditional potato chip manufacturers, declared that every Pringles package would have to carry a boldfaced notice that the product was made from dehydrated potatoes, market share plummeted even more.

In 1979, as he prepared to take over as CEO, Smale declared that Pringles had five years to return to profitable growth. Failing that, the brand would be discontinued.

Changes to the Pringles recipe and to its production process helped revive the brand in the early 1980s, boosting growth enough to keep it off the chopping block. But there was still the matter of the giant production facility in Jackson.

It had been built when P&G was shipping as many as 10 million cases of Pringles every year and expected demand to rise, not fall. But now, the plant was typically running at about 20% of its full capacity, making it virtually impossible to operate at a profit when overhead costs were factored in. In fact, Pringles had cost P&G upwards of $150 million over nearly two decades.

When I spoke with Bob Gill, he told me that meeting with Smale was exciting for several reasons. The promotion to category general manager had been a big step, and he sensed that he would be asked to engineer the turnaround of a brand that had been a drag on the company for almost as long as he had worked there. But the meeting was also meaningful to Gill because of history that he and Smale shared.

Gill explained that, like Smale, he was a graduate of Miami University. Gill had been an underclassman there in the 1970s when Smale, then company president, returned to campus for a talk about Procter & Gamble. Inspired, Gill buttonholed him afterward and asked Smale if he would talk a bit about how his career had developed. Smale obliged the eager young student, mentioning, among other things, that his early experience in sales at the Vick Chemical Co. had been instrumental in helping him succeed at P&G.

"Vicks didn't recruit at Miami anymore, so I chased them down, and I eventually got a traveling sales job at Vicks, similar to Smale's," Gill told me. "I had that first job because of him, because of that little discussion we had. He didn't tell me to do that. I just thought, 'Well, it worked for him. He seems to be doing pretty well. He's from Miami,' and so I did it."

A few years later, after graduate school, he applied for a marketing job at P&G and was given a position on the Gleem toothpaste team — the same brand where Smale had started his P&G career.

Sitting across from Smale in the CEO's office, he told me, he felt as though he had closed some sort of circle and was ready to move on to his next challenge.

They began by discussing the Pringles brand and its history. At that point, Gill had been on the job for about two weeks and was still learning his way around the category. Smale walked him through the details of the Pringles story and the struggle to find profitability.

That Pringles was losing money wasn't news to anyone, and neither was the reason why. Gill wanted to be sure he understood what Smale needed from him, so he decided to be direct.

"John, what do you want me to do?" he asked.

"Well, fill up the capacity, obviously," Smale said.

Gill was taken aback.

"Well, yeah, but they've been trying to do this for almost 20 years," he said. Some of the company's top managers, Ed Artzt and others, had struggled with Pringles to little success.

"Well, that's why you're here, Bob," Smale said. "To fill up the plant."

Gill told me that he had left the meeting in a bit of a daze. "What the heck am I going to do?" he wondered.

It was a strange directive, "Fill up the plant." Smale could as easily have said, "Sell more Pringles." The end result would have been the same. But he hadn't, and Gill began to think about why that was.

He recalled something that Smale had said when he announced the transition to category management: "The category general manager will have direct responsibility for profit, volume, share, cash flow, for the total results of the brands in the category."

If Smale had told him to simply sell more Pringles and how to do it, he'd have been asking Gill to approach the problem like a brand manager. But as a category general manager, he had much more holistic control of the way the Pringles business was run than as a brand manager. Each key function that determined the brand's performance would answer to him: R&D, manufacturing, marketing and finance.

In fact, that was exactly why Smale and Pepper had created the new management system. Gill could implement a new sales strategy if he wanted to. But if research indicated that the formulation of Pringles needed further changes to improve its taste, he could authorize that, too, without consulting a distant group of managers somewhere on the 11th floor. If he wanted to change the packaging, that was his call. If production needed to be streamlined, he could make that happen.

Pringles would be one of the early tests of the category management structure, and over the next several years Gill, and other new category general managers, would demonstrate just how effective the new system was.

Gill and his category team decided to completely rethink the way P&G made and marketed Pringles. They developed a new and better-tasting version of the snack — one that was able to beat market leader Lay's 60-40 in a blind taste test. As a bonus, the change also helped streamline production, further reducing costs.

The reformulation meant that P&G would have run afoul of the Food and Drug Administration if the company continued marketing the product as "potato chips." So, making a virtue of necessity, they decided to change the way Pringles were described on the packaging. No longer would they be "potato chips" — the designation that had prompted the FDA's prominent disclaimer. Going forward, Pringles would be "potato crisps."

Research had revealed that Pringles were far more popular among youth than with adults, so the team focused on an ad campaign that owed much to the style of music video editing that was then dominating the upstart MTV cable network. The result was the award-winning "Once you pop, you can't stop" campaign.

The Pringles turnaround would unfold over a decade, as clever marketing and a broad variety of new flavors turned it into a billion-dollar-a-year success story.

It was evident even in the early years after the switch to category management that stripping away layers of management had infused new energy into the company.

When Smale looked back at the decision, it would be with a mix of pride that it had worked and regret that he hadn't done it sooner.

"It was clear within a year or two that it was working," he said. "In fact, it was clear to me that I should have made that move three or four years before I did. With hindsight, I was later with it than I should have been.

"We were changing conventional wisdom," he continued. "We were going to be doing something differently than it had been done before. There is, at least with many of us, a certain amount of inertia. When you make a major decision like that, and if it's the right decision, then whoever made that decision made it too late."

To be clear, Smale's self-deprecation shouldn't distract from the fact that most people wouldn't have challenged conventional wisdom in the first place. He had the vision to do so, whether he took credit for it or not.

CHAPTER 13

Believing in the Power of Innovation

From the day I began interviewing people about John Smale, they told me constantly about his commitment to innovation and his willingness to take a chance on a long shot, if success meant that the company would solve a major problem for consumers and do it in a way that would strengthen the business.

One day, I sat down with Ceil Kuzma, a former R&D executive with the company, who told me how P&G revitalized its struggling hair-care business in the 1980s, while simultaneously simplifying the lives of millions of women.

By the early 1980s, one of the multiple problems confronting Procter & Gamble was declining market share and profits in women's hair-care products, long one of its most successful market segments.

In a sense, P&G had become a victim of its own success. For decades, many women in the United States had viewed washing and styling their hair as a weekly ritual — something that could take hours as hair, set in curlers, slowly dried into a style that would last for days at a time. P&G, as was its habit, tried to develop products that fit their needs, offering shampoos that achieved excellent results from a once-a-week application.

But by the late 1970s and early 1980s, affordable hand-held blow-dryers were utterly changing the way women cared for their hair. It became possible to wash and style hair daily, if one chose, without investing hours of time. At first, this seemed like fabulous news for P&G: As women went from washing their hair once a week, on average, to five times a week, shampoo use skyrocketed.

By 1981, when Smale took over as CEO, the elation had been replaced by worry about declining market share among P&G's haircare products. The shampoos that did such a good job when used weekly were far too strong for everyday use. Daily washing stripped hair of its natural oils, and frequent blow-drying left some women's hair feeling dried out and brittle.

The answer for many was to add a conditioner to their hair-care routine. Conditioner applied after washing hair had the effect of undoing some of the shampoo's work, depositing enough oily residue to leave hair feeling soft. It was becoming obvious that, as consumer habits changed, shampoos that didn't offer a side-by-side conditioning product would continue to suffer in the marketplace.

P&G, however, was in the business of cleaning things, not getting them dirty again. That fundamental disconnect led to a tense meeting in the conference room down the hall from Smale's 11th floor office in mid-1981.

Ceil Kuzma was at that meeting. She had just been promoted to associate R&D director in the hair-care business — only the second woman in the company's history to reach that level — and it was the first time she had set foot on the 11th floor.

"I was very conscious of the fact that I was the only woman in the room, and I was by far the most junior person," she recalled. "And we were having at the time a very important strategic debate, and John was engaging in that debate. He was causing that debate to happen in front of him. Which was, I thought, a fabulous thing."

Fabulous, that is, until she got pulled into the discussion.

The question at hand was whether P&G should get into the conditioner business. Might it make more sense to sell off its existing brands, except for the market-leading dandruff shampoo Head & Shoulders, and step away from hair care?

The weight of the opinions around the table was in favor of steering clear of conditioners. In 1979, the company had tried to split the difference, adding a conditioning product to a new shampoo, Pert, but the results had been dismal. The conditioning effect was nothing close to what a dedicated conditioner could achieve, and Pert sales stagnated.

Smale looked around the room at the assembled executives from the Hair-Care division, Research & Development and the executive team. From one end of the table to the next, it was the same: men with hair no more than an inch long, who more likely than not used a bar of Ivory Soap to wash it, all of them arguing about women's hair-care products. Except for one person.

At the end of the table sat Kuzma, a petite woman in a navy-blue suit, crisp white shirt and a little bow tie, an outfit she had hoped would help her blend in and perhaps escape notice. No such luck.

"Ceil, you're a woman," Smale said. "What do you think?"

Despite her nervousness, Kuzma laughed to herself. Apparently, the camouflage hadn't worked.

She had fully anticipated getting out of the meeting without saying a word, yet here was the CEO of the company asking her to weigh in on a fight between executives two or three levels more senior than her own boss.

Kuzma took a deep breath. She could sense the mood of the top-level executives in the room, and it was not in favor of starting a new product line in conditioners. The trouble was, she thought they were wrong. And despite her trepidation, she began to tell them why.

A major market need was going unmet, she explained. Women loved the freedom that blow-dryers and new hairstyles gave them from the weekly chore of setting their hair in rollers and sitting around waiting for it to dry. Conditioning products made it possible for them to enjoy that freedom without the negative effects on the health of their hair.

At that point, though, nobody was really producing a good conditioning product. The conditioners on the market left hair feeling softer, yes. But also heavier. And the fatty deposits they left behind adhered to airborne dirt and dust, meaning that conditioned hair got dirty faster.

In other words, this was a technology problem — a space where a company with the ability to innovate could distinguish itself with a superior product.

"We need to learn how to make conditioners," Kuzma said. More importantly, she added, "We need to learn to do conditioning in a shampoo."

This last idea was not new. A two-in-one shampoo-and-conditioner product was practically the Holy Grail in the hair-care business — but nobody, including P&G, had been able to make it work. Shampoos and conditioners were fundamentally different products that worked at cross-purposes. One of them stripped oils from hair, and the other left them behind. Put both in a bottle together, and you wound up with something that did neither very well.

Kuzma had not only contradicted half the P&G executive team, she had also effectively advised Smale to commit the company's R&D resources to a project that had already frustrated some of the best minds in the business.

Whether she knew it at the time or not, Kuzma had cut to the heart of what Smale wanted to see from the P&G research and development organization: an ability to find markets where the introduction of an innovative product could drive big growth and profits, combined with the determination to pursue the research that would make it happen.

The tone in the room immediately changed. Smale began peppering the other executives at the table with questions. Was this really achievable? What was the potential upside? What about the downside?

Kuzma's R&D team, they admitted, had been running a small side project aimed at conquering the two-in-one technology issues. Code-named BC-18, for Beauty Care Product No. 18, it had produced some promising results but was still early in a process that would probably take years and came with no promise of success.

By the time the meeting was over, the change in direction was clear. Procter & Gamble wouldn't just be staying in the hair-care business. If at all possible, it would be revolutionizing it.

Smale's decision to trust Kuzma's instincts on BC-18 would pay extraordinary dividends for P&G, but it took years, and the timely intervention of Gordon Brunner, then a senior R&D executive, to come to fruition.

Kuzma's team successfully formulated the new shampoo but ran into resistance from the company's Beauty Care executives. They weren't sure how to market it and balked at the fact that it would cost more than traditional shampoo. The division's vice president decided not to bring BC-18 to market.

This didn't sit well with Brunner, who at this point was running the Beauty Care Division's R&D operation. He believed that the rewards of success would be so great that the BC-18 project warranted a roll of the dice. He decided to take his case directly to Smale.

Brunner had no direct reporting relationship to the CEO — in fact, it was a breach of normal Procter & Gamble protocol for him to appeal the ruling of a group vice president. Nevertheless, he made an appointment and took the elevator up to the 11th floor.

In the CEO's office, Brunner wasted no time: "This is a fantastic product, John. You've got to give us a chance. Just give us a chance."

Smale was noncommittal. "Okay, Gordon. I'll consider it."

Brunner would later learn that, after he left the office, Smale had walked down to see Bill Connell, who was running the company's shampoo business.

"Bill," Smale said, "get that thing into the market."

Kuzma and her team, it soon became clear, had truly cracked the code of two-in-one products.

The BC-18 technology, in a formulation enriched with vitamins, would eventually be applied to the Pantene line of hair-care products, part of the Richardson-Vicks acquisition. The shampoo's new formulation, combined with a powerful advertising campaign promising "hair so healthy it shines," would turn Pantene into a billion-dollar product, the leading hair-care brand in the world and one of P&G's biggest success stories ever.

It had taken years of work and investment — and a willingness to take a risk on an unproven technology.

That willingness to take the risk, Smale believed, set P&G apart.

"We have a fundamental belief in product innovation," Smale would say years later. "So, we put a lot of emphasis against product innovation, and we focus on it, and we take risks with it. We spend much more money on product development than our competitors. Some of that money is not well spent in the sense that it doesn't produce anything, but that's part of the whole process of investing in innovation. True innovation is generally risk-prevalent."

––––––––––

A different story about an innovation fundamental to Smale's legacy at the company was the development of Liquid Tide, a process that stretched over decades.

When Unilever launched the heavy-duty liquid detergent Wisk in 1956, Procter & Gamble gave it relatively little thought. Less than a decade after launching Tide, P&G was confident in its dominance over the laundry detergent market, and Wisk seemed to present little in the way of a real threat. Unilever was marketing it as a sort of specialty product, anyway — a pre-treatment for stubborn stains.

Without significant resistance from the market leader, Wisk was allowed to develop a foothold, and then to start growing. By the time the detergent's memorable "ring around the collar" advertising tagline was launched in 1968, though, P&G had taken notice.

The problem was that the company really didn't have an answer.

P&G would spend the next decade in an effort to fight its way into the liquid detergent market, trying and failing to challenge Wisk with a series of brands, Tag, Era, and Solo, none of which was able to make a dent.

By the early 1980s, the problem had become acute. Wisk's share of the market was growing, and now approached 10%. For the first time that anybody could remember, Unilever was taking market share away from P&G in the laundry detergent business. P&G was pinning its hopes on a new brand — Omni — and was about to take it to test market when a chemical component of the formula caught the attention of regulators across North America. Soon it was banned in Canada, New York state, and other places, and P&G was left with a new product that it couldn't legally sell in important markets.

The early death of Omni helped push the company in a direction that its leadership, and Smale himself, had been reluctant to explore.

––––––

As part of his push to reinvigorate research and development efforts at P&G, Smale had turned to Wahib Zaki, a brilliant but mercurial scientist who, in the early 1980s, had transformed the P&G's European R&D arm. Zaki appointed Gordon Brunner as his second-in-command, and one of the first projects he handed him was the creation of a new liquid detergent.

It would be the R&D department's first "world" project — meaning that the teams of scientists and researchers that P&G employed across the globe would not be working on a product for their individual markets. They would be pooling their collective expertise in an effort to create a brand that could be manufactured efficiently for multiple marketplaces, only differentiating where necessary to meet local needs.

When Brunner took over, he found that P&G researchers were already well along in the development of a new liquid formula. They were so enthusiastic about it, that they told Brunner that they hoped it would eventually be marketed as "Liquid Tide."

The idea was laughed out of the room whenever it was suggested outside the halls of the R&D department. Tide was a powder. That was part of its brand identity. It was the most popular, best-performing detergent on the market. And furthermore, everybody knew that tests showed powder detergents were still better at getting clothes clean than liquids were, Wisk's popularity notwithstanding.

But Brunner believed in the idea, and he mentioned it to Zaki, who in turn sat down with Smale. He described the global liquid project, and Smale was pleased. It was exactly the kind of thing he had brought Zaki over from Europe to do.

Then Zaki dropped the bombshell. By the way, he said, the R&D department thinks the new liquid ought to be marketed as Liquid Tide.

Zaki knew this wouldn't be an easy sell.

Launching a completely new formulation and a new physical form of its signature brand in a specific category was seen as almost sacrilege at P&G at the time. It was practically gospel that the company would get more growth from introducing a new brand in an established category than it would by modifying an existing brand.

But the company, and John Smale, had also learned the lessons of failing to take breakthrough technology and attach it to its leading brand.

Just a few years before, P&G had developed a new, shaped disposable diaper, which created a snugger, more leak-resistant fit. P&G was already enjoying market leadership in the sector, with Pampers. And although the company recognized the superiority of the new technology, it decided to offer it in a new premium-priced product, Luvs, leaving market-leading Pampers unchanged. It was a disastrous choice, allowing Kimberly-Clark, its biggest competitor in the diaper business, to attack Pampers with a fitted product offered at nearly the same price.

Smale had been president of the company at the time, and he would later concede that it had been one of the company's biggest mistakes on his watch.

When Zaki came to Smale with the idea of a liquid form of Tide, P&G was still fighting to regain the ground it lost in the diaper market, so Smale was attuned to the danger of repeating the Pampers mistake with laundry detergents.

But he wanted to know if the liquid detergent P&G's researchers had developed was truly a breakthrough, on the scale of shaped diapers or fluoride toothpaste, or just an incremental improvement in liquid detergent technology.

The Tide brand name is sacred here, Smale explained. "Try to do it, but I'm not going to accept anything that you propose that won't be a market leader from day one."

Zaki delivered the message to Brunner. There was no way P&G management was going to let a liquid with performance inferior to Tide powder go on the market under the Tide brand.

But as it turned out, the liquid detergent the R&D researchers had invented wasn't just as good as powder Tide at cleaning clothes. In a lot of important respects, it was better. They had even added an innovative convenience feature by developing a self-draining cap for the bottle.

A key moment in the launch of the new product was Brunner's annual product review meeting with Smale. The meeting gave Brunner the chance to pitch the new liquid detergent directly to Smale. "This is a real step forward," Brunner argued. "This is good enough to be Tide."

Advocates of creating a liquid version of Tide soon got the chance to test their theory, when word came down that after meeting with Brunner, Smale had given the go-ahead to a market test.

The results were clear and convincing. The new detergent, marketed as Liquid Tide, outperformed other liquids, not just in the laboratory, but in consumers' washing machines.

One lingering concern was that while Liquid Tide might make inroads against Wisk, it would also cannibalize a certain portion of the market for traditional Tide in powder form. Here, Smale relied not just on his experience with shaped diapers and Crest, but on the even deeper institutional memory instilled in his generation of executives by their predecessors during those daily lunches in the 1960s.

This wouldn't be the first time P&G had launched a breakthrough product that might cannibalize another of its brands. In fact, Tide itself had done just that in the late 1940s. The introduction of the first synthetic detergent was a death sentence for P&G's other laundry brands, but the new technology was so good that the company saw no alternative but to push ahead anyway.

Confronted with the market test results, Smale faced a similar choice. He gave the approval, and the new liquid detergent went to market as Tide.

After Liquid Tide was introduced, a curious thing happened. Within P&G, there was an unspoken desire to crush Wisk, the brand the company had been struggling to overtake for years, but that didn't happen. In fact, for the first two or three years, Wisk didn't surrender any of its market share. But Liquid Tide kept growing. The introduction of a new heavy duty liquid detergent with a recognizable brand name had dramatically expanded the market for liquid detergents in general, and Tide was capturing the bulk of the increase.

————

Ironically, one of the most compelling stories of innovation at P&G during the Smale era relates to a project that he personally tried to kill. Twice.

It was a major effort to reengineer the way the company made paper products, from paper towels to toilet paper to facial tissue. The project's ultimate success, and Smale's willingness to be proved wrong, reveals much about the culture of the company and his comfort in setting aside his own ego for the good of P&G.

By the time Smale became CEO, P&G's Paper Division had become something of a headache for the company. It made a lot of money, but it also cost a tremendous amount of money. Even more than most of P&G's manufacturing operations, the paper business was hugely capital-intensive.

The company's paper mills contained building-size machines that cost millions to design, build, and operate. That made it a difficult business to grow through innovation. Paper products had to be produced at high volume to be profitable and diverting production to test new products cost both time and money.

At the time, Bob Haxby was a senior R&D executive in the Paper Division. His team of scientists had been working on a project known inside the company as CPN, for "confidential product N." It was a new way of making paper that was both stronger and more absorbent — two qualities that didn't normally come together.

If CPN could be made successfully, it would revolutionize all of the company's paper product categories. It would be the kind of quantum leap that Smale always said he wanted from R&D.

But after spending years and hundreds of thousands of dollars, Haxby's team still could not produce CPN paper at scale.

Smale was ready to give up. The paper business just might not be viable for the long term, he said. In fact, Smale had already vowed to other senior executives that P&G would never build another paper machine.

"It's time to shut this down," Smale told Haxby in a product review meeting.

Haxby let Smale know he had heard the message and went back to his office. He asked Paul Trokhan, one of P&G's most prolific inventors and the driving force behind the CPN product, to come see him.

"We've got a problem," Haxby began, and delivered Smale's news. Trokhan was devastated. He believed in CPN as much as he had ever believed in a product at P&G. And he knew that Haxby understood that.

"We have to shut it down?" he asked.

"No," Haxby said. "We've got to go radio-silent on this thing. I don't want you guys to change a thing you're doing. I have confidence in your ability to fix this problem. I don't know what I'll say to John when you come back up aboveground with a success, but I'll think of something."

―――――――

The *Harvard Business Review* once asked Smale whether he ever "vetoed" new product ideas when they were presented to him.

"Occasionally, but not in the abrupt sense usually implied by the idea of vetoing something," he said. "Sometimes I'll say, 'Gee, it seems to me you people are barking up the wrong tree here for this reason or that reason.' If they feel strongly about what they're doing, they'll just go ahead and do it anyway. Six months later or so, the issue will come up again, and eventually it will be resolved on the basis of the evidence."

Seemingly surprised, the interviewer asked, "How do you feel when they 'just go ahead and do it anyway?'"

"All right," Smale said. "I think that's the only way you can operate. I don't know enough about all the issues that involve all the brands and all the categories to be able to make decisions unilaterally. If the decision is clear, then they come to the right decision right away anyway. If it isn't clear, it often involves a thorough understanding of the facts, sometimes more than I have or can get by reading background material. It often involves an instinctive judgment, some of which I can bring.

"But the people directly involved in the product area can and do bring that judgment, and they can be right. History will subsequently indicate that, in some cases, my point of view was wrong and, in others, that it was right."

———————

I asked Haxby how Smale reacted when, a year after being told to shut down the CPN project, he came back to the CEO with the news that Trokhan and his team had produced a successful prototype.

"He never chewed me out. He heard me out," Haxby said. "And he was fair."

What Smale also did was call up Gordon Brunner and ask him to ride herd on the project from then on.

"I want you to get in there," Smale said. "I know you haven't been involved in this, but I want you to get into it. And I want you to tell me what we should do."

Brunner didn't know a lot about the company's paper technology, but he threw himself into the project, taking detailed briefings from P&G's scientists and examining the prototypes that Trokhan's team had designed.

The paper it produced in trials was so clearly superior to what was currently on the market, with its combination of strength, softness and absorbency, that it would give P&G an enormous competitive advantage. The difficulty was that the new kind of paper would require a specialized belt to carry it through the massive paper machines that P&G operated in Mehoopany, Pa. The machines, each one the size of a small building, operated under extreme conditions, generating huge amounts of heat and pressure as they churned out miles of paper every hour. In talking to Haxby and Trokhan, Brunner was convinced they could make a belt that would work.

Reporting back to Smale, Brunner said that the potential payoff from CPN was so great that it justified making what would be a substantial investment. Furthermore, he told Smale, he believed in Haxby and Trokhan.

"John, we can do it," he said.

Smale didn't hesitate. If Brunner believed in it, he said, P&G would provide the resources needed to keep pursuing the breakthrough.

———

On the factory floor in Mehoopany, Trokhan and others working on the CPN product stood anxiously near an enormous paper machine as workers finished installing the belt made for a test run of the new process.

Two hundred feet long and 20 feet wide, this one belt had cost about $100,000 to make. At that price, it needed to run for about 600 hours, or between one and two months of normal operations.

The problem was that the machine it was on was practically designed to tear it apart. The belt would run at more than 2,000 feet per minute, at temperatures exceeding 500 degrees Fahrenheit and under pressures of up to 10,000 pounds per square inch.

As the operators fired up the machine, the researchers held their breath with anticipation. Starting up a paper machine was a process, and it took some time before the various elements got up to speed.

Finally, though, the new belt began moving through the system. After the first few minutes, Trokhan and his colleagues began to allow themselves to hope they had succeeded. Everything was running smoothly, and the new CPN paper came off the belt and headed for the dryer, just as it was supposed to.

After five minutes, hope had turned to excitement. The new belt was working, and Trokhan was already anticipating the potential benefits this new product would have for P&G.

But at around the seven-minute mark, the trouble began. The belt folded over on itself, starting a cascade of catastrophic failures in the machine. Alarms began sounding as the new belt started to come apart, and operators rushed to shut down the machine.

Trokhan told me that the mood went "from elation to total discouragement and dejection seven minutes later."

For more than a year, Trokhan and others struggled to solve the belt-life problem. No matter what they tried, the CPN belts kept breaking.

To Smale, it was beginning to look like a lost cause. The company had spent millions of dollars on the project without finding a way to make CPN paper at scale. And now, sitting on his desk, was a request from Haxby to authorize another $10 million in R&D expenditures. Meanwhile, the market share of P&G's Bounty paper towels had slipped to the mid-20s, and P&G's overall return on investment in the paper business was approaching zero.

At one of the regular briefings Smale received about ongoing R&D efforts, he told Haxby it was time to pull the plug. There would be no going radio-silent this time. Hiding the work of a handful of researchers was one thing, but monopolizing a whole paper machine in Mehoopany and producing $100,000 belts that quickly became scrap was an order of magnitude more expensive.

With John Pepper and Gordon Brunner looking on, Smale delivered the bad news. "Bob, I just don't know how I can agree to this. You're asking for another $10 million or so to keep it going, but belts are still breaking in minutes when they need to run for hours."

Haxby leaned across the table, face to face with the CEO. "John, I want you to trust us," he said. "I want you to trust us. We will make this work. Don't give up now."

Pepper watched Smale's face. Haxby had just made the biggest request a person could make of a manager: asking for trust in the face of repeated and expensive failure.

When I asked John Pepper about that moment, he told me that he had absolutely no doubt about what Smale was about to do. He had watched this play out before, when Smale took Geoff Boisi's advice to raise P&G's offer for Richardson-Vicks. When he had pushed BC-18 shampoo onto the market despite the concerns of the company's Beauty Care executives.

Smale had learned, over years in business, that there were people worth trusting, even when they asked him to go against his own judgment. Haxby, like Boisi, Brunner and Pepper, was one of those people.

"All right, Bob," Smale said, looking back at Haxby. "We'll write the check."

The decision to let Haxby move forward with CPN was trust on a different level. It demonstrated that Smale was willing to see his judgment proved wrong if doing so served the needs of the company.

With the funding secured, Trokhan and his team pressed on, eventually finding a solution that allowed CPN paper to be created on P&G's existing machines.

For P&G, the effect could hardly have been more dramatic. Over the 10 years prior to the introduction of the CPN paper, annual shipments of Bounty paper towels had grown by about 10 million cases. In the 10 years after Smale made that leap of faith, trusting Haxby's team to come up with a solution to the belt problem, sales increased by 32 million cases. Market share, which had bottomed out at 21%, nearly doubled to 41%. Charmin toilet paper went from a 21% share to a 28% share. For both brands, profit margins also increased substantially.

In the space of a few years, P&G had gone from uncertainty about the future of the paper business to enjoying profitable market leadership that would persist for decades.

———

Near the end of his time as CEO, Smale had laid the groundwork for one final effort to solidify the status of R&D as the beating heart of Procter & Gamble.

The idea originated with Brunner, who by this time was not only the chief technology officer at P&G but had been elevated to the board of directors.

As head of R&D, Brunner told me, he was always looking for ways to energize and reward the bench scientists whom the company relied on for new product development. It wasn't always easy.

Among managers at P&G, status was easy to discern — it came with a bigger office, more responsibility, and more visibility within the company. But for scientists at P&G, the trappings of status were a lot harder to see. Many of the company's best minds, Brunner said, were paid as much as managers technically three levels above them, "but [they] couldn't wear their paycheck on their forehead."

Brunner proposed a "society" within the company — one into which only the most accomplished and productive of its research scientists would be inducted. It would be named for Victor Mills, one of the most prolific inventors in the company's history.

This was a huge departure from the norm at P&G, which was still pretty buttoned-down when it came to elevating individuals above their peers outside the company hierarchy.

I asked Brunner how he pitched the idea to Smale.

"I said, the top people, the thing they most care about is being recognized by their peers," he told me. "You can give them money. You can give them a lot of things, they're all nice, but when they're recognized in their peer group as the very best, there's nothing more rewarding."

The idea appealed to Smale for the same reason that Pepper's effort to create a company statement of "Purpose, Values and Principles" had. If a company is upfront about what it values, it's likely to get more of it, whether that's managers willing to take some risks or inventors driving to discover the next breakthrough product.

The inaugural class of Victor Mills Society members was inducted less than a year later, shortly after Smale's retirement. The ceremony was held at the convention center in Cincinnati, in front of the whole P&G organization, whether there in person or on telecast around the globe. Recipients arrived with their entire families and were presented gold medals as their accomplishments were recited for the entire company to hear.

"It was tremendously energizing," Brunner said. "It was the biggest deal we've done for individuals in the history of the company. So, it had this tremendous impact of motivation," he added, letting them see that "the company really did care about people who did big things."

I asked Paul Trokhan, whose research had reinvigorated the company's paper business, about the impact of what most people at P&G now shorthand as the "Vic Mills Society."

Trokhan was one of the inaugural members of the society. Now in his 70s, he was still working at a secure P&G research facility in Cincinnati when he met with me.

"I think it's had a profound impact," he said of the creation of the society. "It's extraordinarily aspirational to people." Thirty years after his own induction, he added, he sees it as "the highlight of my career at Procter & Gamble."

I thought back to my meeting with Kathy Fish, P&G's former chief technology officer, and remembered that Smale had not stopped at laying the groundwork for the Victor Mills Society. Rather, he had created a second award, for young, up-and-coming technologists at the company, funded with a donation of his company stock.

The meaning behind the recording she had played for me — the first time I had ever heard Smale's voice — seemed clearer now than when I first heard it.

I went back to my archive of interviews and played it back again.

"It's important that the people in R&D understand the enormous importance of what they do, because it really is everything we are," Smale said. "We are an R&D-based company. We're a company whose progress and fortunes are based on the success of inventing new brands, new processes that are really distinctive — that are market-changers and really revolutionize a market when we go into it."

He added, "Fundamentally, this is an R&D company. If this company is going to be successful 50 years from now, it will be successful for the same reason that it is now, and that's because we are ahead of the world in almost every category and product innovation."

CHAPTER 14

Knowing Who to Trust

In that period over the summer of 2019, after I had agreed to write a book about John Smale, but before I began researching it in earnest, I had been surprised by the wave of emails that crashed into my inbox after John Pepper put out a request for stories about the former CEO.

Most were channeled toward me via Paul Fox and Ed Tazzia, two key figures in the globe-spanning P&G alumni network.

In addition, I had letters that Smale had received when he retired, when he fell ill with pulmonary fibrosis, and others sent to his family after his death.

The number of people who took the time to write detailed descriptions of what were, in some cases, only brief moments of contact with Smale, now decades in the past, should have signaled something to me.

But I was looking past them. At the time, I saw the stories as interesting, but not necessarily relevant to the larger purpose of telling the story of Smale's career.

Returning to them now, though, I saw them differently. It made me think of the avalanche of emails my father had received after letting his friends and family know he had entered hospice care. The stories people told me about Smale demonstrated the indelible impression he had made on them and how, to many of them, he personified the idealized version of the company they worked for.

Some of the stories I reread demonstrated a deep capacity for empathy that spoke to Smale's belief that commitment to Procter & Gamble meant a commitment to its people — not just its business.

He saw it as vital to maintaining the "soul" of Procter & Gamble, as a place where talented people would be willing — even eager — to spend that "working life." Caring for employees, right down to how managers delivered criticism and set expectations, was "perhaps the most important part of P&G's character," Smale once remarked.

"If we ever lose that, if we ever stop caring about each other, we stop cooperating. If we stop caring about each other, we lose our common vision, our sense of purpose, our commitment to the success of our company," he said. "And should that ever happen, this company will no longer be unique among the world's business organizations."

One story that particularly stood out came from Susan Tiemeier, who had been working for John Smale for about three years when, in the summer of 1980, she nervously knocked at the door to his office and asked to speak with him privately.

Like everyone else at P&G, Tiemeier knew that Smale would soon be running the entire company as chief executive. It had been a major promotion when she was selected to join his administrative support team. But as she stood in front of his desk, she worried that she was about to lose her job.

Tiemeier was in Smale's office to share some deeply personal news: At age 29 and unmarried, she was pregnant.

In a conservative culture like P&G's, Tiemeier felt sure that it would be seen as highly inappropriate for a single mother to work in the office of the CEO. Before Smale could say anything, she offered to resign her position on his staff and return to the regular secretarial pool.

"Sue," Smale said, "we're your friends, and you're going to need your friends now more than ever. I wouldn't think of asking you to leave."

After a moment's reflection, he added, "There's going to be a lot of talk among some of the women on the floor, and you're just going to have to overlook it. Just think of next spring, when you're holding that little baby in your arms, how much joy you're going to feel."

The following year, when Tiemeier's daughter, Jane, was born, she had to spend more than a week in the neonatal intensive care unit. At that time, John and Phyllis Smale made a point of visiting the hospital to assure Tiemeier — correctly, as it turned out — that Jane would be fine and that Tiemeier's job would be waiting for her when she was ready to return to work.

The situation showed a side of Smale that those who knew him only as a tough boss or a sharp business mind might not have expected. But those who knew him well understood that he cared for other P&G employees deeply and believed that, if the company was in a position to help them through a difficult time, it was obligated to do so.

———

The stories about Smale that his former colleagues wanted to share went beyond isolated acts of kindness. Among other things, they showed a man who was compelled to seek out talent within the ranks of P&G, to make sure it was nurtured and allowed to flourish.

Paul Polman, the former chief executive officer of P&G's historical competitor, Unilever, told me that he viewed that trait as one of the keys to Smale's success.

Polman, who spent the first 27 years of his business career at P&G, said that his exposure to Smale during that time convinced him of the importance of investing the time and effort to cultivate younger colleagues.

"John understood, frankly better than anybody else I have met in my career, the power of investing in people as a driver of the success of an organization," Polman said.

A perfect example of that is what happened when word got back to Smale that a young product designer had stood up in a meeting to criticize the company's disastrous decision not to apply its new fitted diaper technology to Pampers, its flagship brand in that market.

The significance of P&G's tactical error on fitted diapers was only just becoming clear when Tamara Minick, a young employee in the Paper Division, was asked to introduce herself at a staff dinner and to tell everyone what she was working on.

Minick dutifully gave her name and said that she was working on the design for a breathable cuff on the still-rectangular Pampers product.

"That project is important to us," the division head said. "What do you think of it?"

"I think we're putting bells and whistles on an Edsel," she replied, referring to the failed Ford car line.

The comment provoked an immediate argument around the table, but Minick held her ground. Consumers consistently said they preferred shaped diapers to rectangular ones by a 2-to-1 margin. Putting breathable cuffs on Pampers wasn't going to change that.

At home that night, Minick called her father and told him about the conversation. "I probably just lost my job," she said, glumly.

"Well, did you believe what you said?" her father asked.

"Yes."

"If you get fired over that, you're in the wrong place anyway."

The next morning, Minick's phone rang, but it wasn't the HR department telling her to pack up her desk. It was a secretary in John Smale's office. The details of her comments had been relayed to the CEO, and he wanted her to prototype a shaped version of Pampers. He needed five of them on his desk by Monday.

Working around the clock with a P&G technician named Virginia Bowles, Minick produced the diapers by hand, and within a few days, Smale had authorized $5 million to build a test line for the new diaper.

Before long, Smale would finally make the call to shift Pampers to an hourglass design, a move that entailed half a billion dollars in capital expenditures, to build new production facilities, and another $225 million in marketing.

Minick had assumed that her brief interaction with John Smale had been a one-off occurrence. However, it wasn't long before their paths crossed again.

A few months later, Minick took part in a group meeting between Smale and a number of engineers. At one point, Smale asked the group, "What do you see your obligation to this company to be?"

Minick spoke from the heart, and shortly afterward, Smale would quote her directly in the year-end speech he delivered to company management.

> What, I said, do you see your obligation to this company to be? One of the answers I got is worth repeating here.
>
> This person said that their obligation was to develop the "big product edge," to bring innovative technology to the product or product area for which they were responsible. Innovation that would truly distinguish that product from competitive products in the marketplace in its ability to provide the consumer with meaningfully better product performance.
>
> The comment didn't end there, however.
>
> This person went on to say that, besides being obligated to the company for a truly innovative product, they were obligated to be a champion of that innovative idea, to believe in it, nurture it, and work as hard as they could to convince others of its value.
>
> In a sense, that person was establishing a standard of excellence, saying this is what the company has a right to expect from my work. And this is what I expect from my work.
>
> We all have that same obligation.

Smale was so impressed by Minick that he arranged quarterly lunches with her, asking her to speak with him, she recalled, about "anything I wanted with regard to the company: my projects, questions about the broader company."

He eventually guided her into the marketing side of the business, a move that would eventually vault Minick beyond P&G, to increasingly senior jobs with Cadbury, Elizabeth Arden and Pearson, before she eventually founded her own company.

Minick's experience with Smale was not unique. His talent for developing future leaders and inspiring them by example would echo through the business world for decades.

Janet Reid was the first black woman with a Ph.D. to be hired in one of P&G's technical fields when she brought her degree in bioinorganic chemistry to the company's Food and Beverage Division in 1980.

Reid had never met John Smale and, as a relatively junior employee in a technical field, she had little expectation she ever would. But she still felt a personal connection to the CEO because of his service on the board of the United Negro College Fund. Reid's father had been president of Dillard University in New Orleans, and Reid herself had done her training at Howard University in Washington, D.C. Both Dillard and Howard are historically black universities with deep connections to the UNCF.

Several years after Reid joined the company, her supervisor invited her to an event in Cincinnati at which P&G had purchased a table. To her surprise, she found herself sitting by Smale. They struck up a conversation that continued throughout the evening. Reid thanked him for his work on the UNCF board, and Smale pressed for details about her work with the company.

Reid assumed the dinner was the beginning and end of her relationship with Smale, but the next day, her supervisor got a call from the CEO. He wanted Reid transferred out of R&D into brand management. It was part of a companywide effort to move promising people between divisions, to seed new thinking and help different parts of the company understand each other better.

Over the next several years, Smale would keep track of Reid, inviting her to lunch on the 11th floor once or twice a year in a relationship that would continue until his retirement.

After 10 years at P&G, Reid left to form her own company, which grew into Global Novations, a management consulting firm ultimately acquired by Korn Ferry International. She now runs BRBS World LLC, a global management consultancy based in Cincinnati.

"All along this journey at P&G, I kept seeing the power of inclusion, diversity and equity when it is part of the culture of a corporation," Reid wrote. "John Smale first demonstrated to me the power of thinking differently and fostering inclusion, diversity and equity."

———

Another theme that arose frequently in those emails was trust. Specifically, that Smale demonstrated, time and again, his willingness to trust people to grow and develop.

John Pepper had tried to explain this to me when we first met. I had asked him about the first time he met Smale.

It had been a car ride, he answered. Both men had been attending a presentation by the advertising agency Young & Rubicam at a Cincinnati hotel. Smale, then a group vice president in charge of multiple divisions of P&G, offered Pepper a ride back to headquarters.

Pepper had been with the company for more than a decade at that point but was still multiple levels below Smale on the P&G org chart, a huge difference, given the then-rigid hierarchy of the company. The two almost never crossed paths. But Pepper knew exactly who Smale was — a rapidly rising executive who seemed destined for a top slot in the organization.

"I'd never really been with him in a one-on-one situation before, business or otherwise," Pepper told me. "He got in the car and he said, 'What do you think of that presentation we just heard?' I said, I thought it was really terrible. It just made no sense to me."

As it happened, Smale had thought the presentation was awful, too, but what Pepper would remember from the exchange — in addition to the relief he felt at finding they agreed — was that Smale had actually cared what he thought.

"I've remembered ever since — he was actually interested in my opinion," he told me.

It was also the first step in Smale assessing Pepper. Was this a man whose judgment he could trust? Pepper may not have been in a senior position yet, but he was clearly on that track. That seemingly innocuous question during a brief drive across Cincinnati had been an opening probe in a relationship — one that would have a mentoring quality and ultimately evolve into a close friendship over the coming decades.

Pepper told me that he would remember that car ride years later, while heading P&G's operations in Europe. At the time, he was concerned that the company had yet to release a liquid laundry detergent in that market.

A liquid product in the pipeline, called Vizir, was suitable for European machines, but Pepper was having a hard time getting approval to launch it. Product launches were expensive, and the company's profits were under immense pressure that year.

Pepper sent a proposal to Smale, who turned it down. Then he sent another, with some improvements. Again, Smale rejected it.

Pepper was convinced that Henkel, one of P&G's major competitors in Europe, was on the verge of releasing a heavy-duty liquid and forcing P&G to play catch-up. He was damned if he was going to see that happen.

So, for a third time, he sent the proposal back to Cincinnati, and this time the result was a phone call with Smale and Ed Artzt, who was supporting Pepper's recommendation to go ahead.

"I guess we put you in that job," Smale said. "I guess the point in time has come where we better follow what you want to do."

Pepper would often cite those 25 words and the effect they had on him at the time. The confidence Smale expressed in him in that moment echoed through the coming decades of Pepper's career.

"That means the world to anybody," he told me.

————————

Smale also understood that people needed to be allowed to grow into new responsibilities, to work through mistakes and to be allowed to recover from them. In other words, to earn back his trust. One of the people who made that clear to me was Charlotte Otto.

Otto had come to P&G in 1976 after graduating from business school at Purdue. She was part of the first class of new marketing hires to include a significant share of women. In 1983, Otto transferred to the Paper Division, where she took on increasing responsibilities.

After she was tapped to sit on a task force focused on P&G's efforts to increase diversity, she attracted Smale's attention. He was on the lookout for fresh talent to help lead the company's approach to emerging issues such as environmental protection and animal testing.

Not long afterward, Otto's manager called her into his office to tell her that John Smale wanted her to move to a new position in Public Affairs responsible for "issues management."

Otto told me she was devastated at the prospect of being sent to what she considered a corporate backwater.

Her immediate boss countered that this was a plum assignment. After all, the CEO had asked for her. Unpersuaded, she went to talk with John Pepper, who was then the head of U.S. business. She told him that being asked to take this assignment outside of the business line made her feel like "damaged goods."

Pepper was shocked that she was resisting a role that Smale had specifically selected her for.

"Go try it," he said. "If you don't like it, you've got a return ticket."

The Public Affairs division was unfamiliar ground for her, but she was told that senior management — meaning Smale — wanted her to get hands-on experience in the job, with an eye to running the division in the future.

To start, she was handed a project directly from Smale. He and a number of other CEOs in the consumer products sector were concerned about the growing movement to ban the testing of new products on animals. Their coalition had agreed in principle to work toward a future in which no animal testing was required but did not commit to an immediate cessation. Their position was that, until an alternative was available, animal tests were essential to protecting human health.

"I've laid the groundwork, so why don't you get your counterparts together and develop a coalition that will sponsor an industry-wide program to protect our right to test on animals," he told Otto.

"Okay, I'm up to that," she thought. She drafted a letter that laid out what the coalition could accomplish and how much money it would cost. The letter was peppered with specific references to Smale and, without thinking much about it, Otto sent it out to the public affairs officers at other companies.

A few days later, her phone rang. It was a reporter with the *Cincinnati Enquirer*, asking about John Smale's advocacy of animal testing. Otto's heart sank. She would later learn that the secretary of her counterpart at Unilever had leaked the letter to an animal rights group, which had in turn sent it on to the press.

The coalition was to be a joint effort by multiple companies, including P&G, Unilever, Johnson & Johnson, 3M and others. But Smale's name was the only one on the letter, which made him the immediate target of animal rights organizations across the country. A media firestorm erupted, including a story leading the business section of the *Cincinnati Enquirer* that pointed out Smale's personal involvement in the group.

A few days later, Otto's phone rang, and Smale's secretary put the CEO on the line.

"Hi, John," Otto said.

"It seems we have some issues," Smale began.

"Yes," Otto said grimly.

"Tell me what happened," Smale said.

Otto had been thinking about nothing else and rattled off her mistakes as she saw them. She had failed to consider the different viewpoints of people who might see the letter. She had put in writing things that might better have been handled in a discussion. And she had made the CEO of P&G the public face of a campaign that had been meant to provide the consumer product industry with the safety of numbers.

Otto finished, nearly certain that she was about to be fired.

"Well, it sounds like you've learned a lesson," Smale said.

Otto was momentarily nonplussed. "Oh, indeed I have, John. I've learned a lot of them."

"Well, good," Smale said. "Thank you." And he hung up.

Otto went on to lead the Public Affairs division, and in 1996, she became P&G's first female corporate officer. She retired as global external relations officer in 2010. Throughout her career, she said, she never forgot that brief phone call with the CEO.

"I never heard about it again," she told me. "It could have been a black mark on my career. The way John Smale handled this said so much about the man and the company. It changed my attitude on how you handle mistakes: Don't shoot the messenger; learn from experience."

Since trust seemed so fundamental to Smale's decision-making process, I naturally wondered how he decided whom he could trust. One thing I was sure of was that, when it came to his colleagues at P&G, Smale started with a baseline assumption of good faith just because they were at P&G in the first place.

"I think our character is unambiguous enough so that we attract certain kinds of people who get into the company, and are comfortable with and like this kind of an environment," he once said. "They like the challenge that it represents. They want to be working with people who have got high, lofty goals, who want to be leaders whether they're in product development or marketing, et cetera. That's a characteristic, an aura of the company that goes on from generation to generation, at least from the days of [former P&G leaders] McElroy and Morgens on. There are certainly other companies who do very, very well and are key leaders in their industries, so I'm not trying to suggest that we are somehow unique, but I think that the genesis of the foundation of what creates a Procter & Gamble is this kind of a character, this kind of a personality."

But even within P&G, people aren't interchangeable. Not everyone is a good fit for every job. How did Smale decide, as he must have done thousands of times, that he had the right person in a specific position? That he could trust them to make the right decision? That they would do the right thing?

A hint came to me in the form of an email from Mick Yates, a former senior manager in P&G's European business.

When Smale retired, Yates said, he took the opportunity at a reception to ask him about something that many former P&G people had mentioned: Smale's uncanny ability to wrong-foot even the company's most experienced managers with an unanticipated question.

In his job, Smale said, he would meet with hundreds of P&G managers every year. He couldn't hope to know everything about their projects and didn't normally have time to look at extensive briefing materials that they often brought with them. What he needed to know most of all was whether he could trust them to do the job he needed them to do.

So, over the years, he had developed what he thought of as his "piece of string" theory.

Any manager that got to the point of meeting with the CEO at P&G was going to be smart and experienced, he told Yates, so the first question he asked would always be a test. It would be something that couldn't be answered by reference to a spreadsheet or a set of talking points, something that required a deep familiarity with a specific project to answer coherently.

That first question was the "piece of string" in Smale's theory, and in asking it, he began to pull. Did the person in front of him know their stuff? If they did, Smale usually let it go and listened to the rest of the presentation.

If they didn't, though, he kept pulling. Could they be honest about not knowing an answer? Did they know enough about their own project to be able to think on their feet? One question would lead to a second, and perhaps a third.

"Eventually, either the ball of string holds tight, or it totally unravels," Smale explained.

In his email, Yates had made the point of saying that Smale, in his questioning, was never unkind or nasty. But that didn't make being on the receiving end of his piece-of-string test any less unsettling. Some, in fact, found facing his probing questions and clipped comments even more intimidating than dealing with other bosses who simply shouted when they were unhappy.

It occurred to me that what Smale was looking for wasn't just raw brainpower — it was a balance of commitment and integrity. He wanted people who shared his mastery of the details of P&G's business and his passion for winning. People so focused on success that they looked past the immediate challenges their business was facing and worried about things that hadn't happened yet.

The people who could answer the questions in Smale's piece-of-string test were the ones so committed to success that they never stopped thinking about it.

Smale was looking for people who held themselves to the same standard he held himself.

As for Yates, he had found himself intrigued by Smale's explanation, but unsatisfied.

"Yes, John," he said. "But how did you decide on the first question?"

"Ah, Mick," Smale smiled. "That's the trick."

———

Chris Caldemeyer gave me another way of thinking about how his grandfather assessed people. Chris had the good fortune to accompany Smale on many fishing trips, frequently to exclusive properties and remote lodges, where, at the end of the day, high-powered business leaders and other highly successful people found themselves gathered with nothing to do but talk to each other.

Chris, in his early teens, had little to contribute to conversations between the CEOs of major companies, but he had the writer's gift of observation. What he saw from his grandfather was, primarily, silence.

In a room full of people who loved to hear themselves talk, Smale was reticent, Chris remembered, never offering opinions for their own sake but always assessing, learning and remembering.

"I think that restraint helped him probably learn more," Chris said. "And it also kept him a little bit mysterious, too. This guy, he's not talking, so when he does speak, you listen. When John Smale spoke, people got quiet and listened to him."

I pressed Chris on this. What was his grandfather trying to gauge when he spent all that time listening to other people talk? What did he want to understand about them?

It was, Chris thought, about authenticity. His grandfather, Chris told me, had an uncanny ability to see through the veneers people construct as they move through the world, and to assess what he believed were their real motivations.

"It was like he had the ability to determine the authenticity of someone's actions," he told me. "And if somebody was inauthentic, he had a very hard time stomaching that."

It seemed to me that, in Smale's mind, authenticity must have been a necessary component of the kind of commitment he demanded of himself and of the people around him. Without it, dedication to the job was nothing more than a front, put forward for managers to see, but not reflective of true dedication to the work.

When I started researching this book, I had been genuinely surprised at how adamant current and former P&G employees were about the company being different from most other businesses. It made more sense to me now, though.

Smale's daughter, Lisa, told me that her father believed so deeply in the exceptional character of the company that he had, in some way, infused it into his children when they were young.

"To him it wasn't about the money; he was part of an enterprise that he adored, and he just felt so strongly about the morals of the company," she told me.

It went so deep that, when she got older and started to hear complaints about rapacious corporations placing profit above all else, she at first didn't understand how that was possible.

Inside P&G, Smale could convince even the most junior people in the company that they were an indispensable part of an important and ongoing enterprise — one bigger than themselves.

And the themes that arose so frequently in those emails about Smale, caring for each other and mutual trust, made this perfectly clear.

A majority of the P&G people I met spoke of their time with the company in the same way former athletes or members of the military speak of their careers. They remember a time when they felt that they were part of something larger than themselves, part of a team where their individual contribution was not only appreciated but recognized as essential to the overall success of the enterprise.

In an interview with *Cincinnati Magazine* in the 1980s, Smale had elaborated on the kind of people he thought were attracted to P&G and how he personally felt about them.

"I think you could characterize P&G people in a way, by their own character," he said. "I think, by and large, they are people who want to work, have a work ethic about them, want to do the work they do to the standard of excellence and who have a sense of identification and affection for the relationship they have with this organization. The company, yes. But also with the people in the company."

Tapping the identification badge that he wore on his chest while on P&G grounds, he said, "When I see people with one of these ID badges on, I know they're part of the Procter & Gamble organization, and in my mind, I figure they must be pretty good people."

CHAPTER 15

A Commitment to Cincinnati

Between the voluminous records in the P&G archives and ongoing interviews with Smale's former colleagues and employees, I had assembled an extensive record of what he had accomplished at P&G during the decade he served as CEO. But one thing I wanted to get a better sense of was Smale's connection to the city of Cincinnati.

On one of my trips to the city, Cathy Caldemeyer had walked me through Smale Riverfront Park, a complex of gardens, performance spaces and public recreation areas. Her father had donated $20 million to the city to provide initial funding for the park, which reclaimed 32 acres of disused land along the banks of the Ohio River.

Smale had intended the park to be a monument to Phyllis and for the complex to be named for her. After he died, though, Cathy prevailed on the city to change the official name to the John G. and Phyllis W. Smale Riverfront Park. She knew it would have annoyed her father, but she did it anyway, figuring that he deserved the recognition.

I knew, though, that despite its prominence in the public eye, the park was only a small part of what Smale did for Cincinnati. In the 1980s, while CEO of P&G, he had been drafted to chair a commission charged with utterly overhauling the infrastructure of the city.

Cincinnati was once renowned for its expansive network of public parks. But by 1986, it had been forced to close many of them because of a lack of funds to maintain them. Streets were pocked with potholes; bridges and viaducts were in an alarming state of disrepair; and the sewer and water systems relied on pipes laid down more than a century before.

That August, a sewer pipe that had been in place since the Johnson administration — the Andrew Johnson administration — collapsed, taking part of the road near Riverfront Stadium with it.

The road closure restricted access to the stadium that was home to two of the city's great unifying institutions, Major League Baseball's Cincinnati Reds and the National Football League's Cincinnati Bengals. The resulting mess felt like a symbol of everything that was wrong with the city.

The man I needed to talk to was Charlie Luken, who had been the 34-year-old mayor of Cincinnati at the time.

We met downtown, in the offices of his law firm, but before we dug into the details of what became known as the Smale Commission, Luken wanted to tell me a story.

In the mid-1980s, during Luken's first term as mayor, he frequently drove downtown along Columbia Parkway, a stretch of U.S. 50 that snakes along a bluff high above the Ohio River. Often, when he came to the spot where Torrence Parkway dumped commuters from Cincinnati's upscale residential neighborhoods onto the highway, he'd spot a woman on her hands and knees in the dirt along the shoulder, wearing work gloves and scratching away at the earth with gardening tools. He began seeing her in other places, too, planting flowers and shrubbery in public spaces, apparently on her own initiative.

"I'd be like, 'Who is this lady with the gloves planting flowers in a public right-of-way?'" he said. "Well, it was Phyllis Smale."

It was certainly of a piece with everything I had heard about Phyllis from her children. Jay Smale, John and Phyllis's oldest son, once told me that during a brief and unsuccessful attempt by the Smale family to learn to play golf, he had turned around to find his mother weeding the tee box.

Luken, distressed by the city's crumbling infrastructure and the inability of the dysfunctional City Council to do anything about it, had persuaded council members and the city manager to let him take the case to those with the most obvious stake in Cincinnati's well-being, its business leaders.

He envisioned a commission made up of top business figures who could study the city's problems, propose solutions and, most importantly, put their considerable influence behind a campaign to make the city follow through on a comprehensive infrastructure project.

But Luken, a Democrat in a city where the business community was staunchly Republican, knew he wasn't the ideal messenger. Infrastructure updates would involve tax increases, and in the Ronald Reagan era, when the GOP firmly believed that government was the cause of most problems, not the solution, a Democratic mayor calling for tax hikes wouldn't get past the secretary of any businessman in town.

Only one person in the city had the pull to bring together the business community behind such an effort, Luken said.

"My thought was, if this was going to be successful, we would need the CEO of Procter & Gamble," he said.

Luken met with Smale at P&G headquarters and made his pitch. He didn't know Smale well, but he said he was struck by the intensity with which the CEO listened to him. "John was a really good listener," he said, even while admitting that he wasn't sure, at the time, what Smale was thinking.

One meeting led to another, and Smale considered the idea.

"I think he was at first a little reluctant," Luken said. "Not because he didn't want to help the city. But because he wasn't sure he wanted to get involved in the quandary that is city politics."

———

What Luken may not have understood at the time was that other factors were at play.

P&G was preparing to celebrate the 150th anniversary of its founding in 1986, and the company was becoming much more intentional in its relationship with the city of Cincinnati.

Over the years, the company had actively donated both money and its executives' time to the city. It was clear to Smale, as it had been to his predecessors, that an investment in Cincinnati was also an investment in the company.

"We hire people from all over the country and ask them to move here and raise their families here," Smale once said. "It needs to be a good place. A place where people want to live."

Like other P&G leaders before him, Smale had taken on broad responsibilities outside his role with the company. There was a sort of unwritten rule at P&G that executives were expected to play a civic role, as well as a business role.

In a 1982 article, the *Cincinnati Enquirer* noted that "one would be hard pressed to find an established board, committee, commission or cause without someone from P&G on it. From the Cincinnati Symphony board to the Fine Arts Fund, the Cincinnati Business Committee to hospital and university boards, the Red Cross, Junior Achievement, the Cincinnati Zoo and steering committees of the Democratic, Republican and Charter parties, P&G is represented."

———————

When Smale signed on, Luken was not fully prepared for what he would get. First of all, Smale reassigned several high-level P&G executives to work full time on the business of the commission.

"I remember that first year, I thought, 'If I have one more meeting with a Procter & Gamble executive ... .' I was getting kind of up to here with it," Luken said, holding his hand level with his throat.

Luken, a big-picture person, wanted to delegate the responsibility for details, but the Procter & Gamble people working on the project were, like Smale, obsessive about them.

"He wanted to get in the weeds of, you know, what's the sewer capacity of pump number three and station number 10? He wanted all this very, very documented."

Smale called on his contacts and friends across the Cincinnati business community to join the growing effort.

One was Charlie Mechem, Smale's friend and the chairman and CEO of Cincinnati-based media conglomerate Taft Broadcasting. Mechem didn't think twice.

"If John asked you to do something and you had no good reason not to, you'd do it," Mechem said. "Because you knew that he wouldn't undertake anything frivolous."

From August through early November, Smale laid the groundwork for an unprecedented top-to-bottom review of the city and its needs. In addition to Mechem, he pulled in executives from Federated Department Stores, General Electric, the Kroger supermarket chain, Cincinnati Bell and other businesses with a large local presence.

In November 1986, the official launch of the City of Cincinnati Infrastructure Commission took place in a packed hotel ballroom during a lunch sponsored by the Chamber of Commerce. Speaking to approximately 1,000 members of the local business community, Smale outlined his plan for a year-long effort to identify the city's needs and to develop a proposal to address them, both operationally and financially.

Outside the event, Luken was challenged by a reporter about the decision to hand off responsibility for studying essential city services to a nongovernmental commission, headed by a business executive. The young mayor was blunt. "The fact of the matter is, we're in bad shape and we need some help, and he's providing the leadership that we need," Luken said of Smale.

Inside, Smale went to the podium. Having already secured the cooperation of the top leaders of some of the city's largest employers, he made the case to the rest of the city's business community to get involved.

The commission would have five subcommittees, covering streets and roads, parks and recreation, buildings, water and sewers, and funding. Co-chairs of the five subcommittees were a who's who of Cincinnati's corporate leaders. Each subcommittee would have subcommittees of its own, creating ample opportunity for business leaders to offer time and expertise to the effort.

"I firmly believe that government care and private care must go hand in hand to make this happen," Smale said. "What I'm saying is that I believe each of us must take a more active role as individuals and as business leaders to restore the full beauty of our city that was such a great source of pride to us only a few years ago."

A year after it was launched, the Smale Commission — as it was now being called by virtually everyone — delivered a comprehensive report with a plan to completely overhaul city infrastructure. The 100-point set of recommendations stretched over parts of three pages when it was printed in the *Cincinnati Enquirer*, touching on everything from sewers to roads to solid waste disposal.

It called for more than $10 billion in spending. And, crucially, the commission report recommended increased user fees for city amenities and a new tax on Cincinnati workers, equivalent to one dollar for every $1,000 in income.

Smale had insisted on a provision that would prevent the city from doing anything with the tax revenue other than what it was expressly intended for. None of the money collected under the new revenue measures would be dispensed to the city, except when it was directed to the infrastructure projects the commission had identified and to the future maintenance of those projects. Another condition was that none of the money would be available to the city unless the level of other spending on infrastructure in a given year met an inflation-adjusted minimum.

"It was the genius of it, really," Luken told me. "He wasn't going to let us take this money and squander it on something else."

Some members of the city council were less than pleased with proposals for higher taxes and increased fees for parking, and they seemed prepared to dismiss the commission's proposal almost immediately. That prompted a blistering editorial from the *Enquirer*, which pointed out that it was years of neglect by that same city council that had brought the city's infrastructure to its current state of disrepair.

"If the Smale Commission has its way," the editorial said, "Cincinnati will not only catch up, but also commit itself to a program of continuing maintenance so that the next generation of Cincinnatians will not be confronted with the kind of neglect and deterioration that faces this one."

Still, there was considerable opposition to the proposal, and its fate was ultimately deferred to the public, through a referendum scheduled to take place about 18 months after the Smale Commission officially launched.

Smale took an unusually public stance on the measure, drafting an op-ed for the *Enquirer* in support of the ballot measure, which had come to be known as "Issue One" in Cincinnati.

"At its root, this is really an economic development proposition — economic development, not just because of the jobs which will be created in the process of fixing up and maintaining the city's infrastructure," Smale wrote. "But because a more attractive Cincinnati means a more competitive Cincinnati — a Cincinnati that will attract and keep more jobs.

"This is a 'win-win' situation — a good deal for Cincinnati and a good deal for Cincinnatians. It's an opportunity to make this city truly unique among the cities of this country."

Smale also undertook a less obvious role in the campaign to get the measure passed. That spring, Cincinnatians who turned on their televisions saw an advertisement calling on them to support Issue One. It featured a close-up shot of a pothole filled with muddy water, as car and truck tires repeatedly slammed into it.

"The streets of Cincinnati are a problem," a narrator said. "We all know. We all want them fixed. Now there is a low-cost way. On May 3, vote for Issue One. Issue One guarantees right in the ballot language that every dollar will be used for streets, bridges, parks, recreation areas and other portions of the city's infrastructure. You can make sure that our streets and bridges are repaired and maintained by voting for Issue One. Let's do it now. On May 3, vote for Issue One."

The advertisement closed with an image of the pothole suddenly filled, and a car tire preparing to drive smoothly across it. Along the bottom of the screen, in tiny type, was the notice that the spot had been paid for by an organization called Citizens for Better Streets & Bridges.

This was a newly organized group, boasting a phone number that spelled out the world P-O-T-H-O-L-E. The organization's three chairs included Theodore Berry, an attorney and former mayor, and Sister Anne Rene McConn, a Catholic nun, neither of whom had any particular expertise in advertising. The third member of the board was John Smale.

In the end, the effort was enough. Just barely. The votes in favor totaled 50.2% of the ballots, with opposition at 49.7%.

Luken told me that he had seen Issue One's passage as a tribute to Smale's credibility with the people of Cincinnati: "People trusted the CEO of Procter more than they trusted the political establishment."

"The city owes him a great debt of gratitude that lives today," the former mayor added. "He made a mark that very few will ever make, in terms of being a giant of Cincinnati. Smale Park is probably the most obvious reflection of it, but everything from the water we drink to the sewer plants to the roads and bridges, you know, he's got a little piece of all of that."

CHAPTER 16

Sharing Successes

The first iteration of this book tried to capture a series of moments that illustrated and defined Smale's character. What is a life, after all, but a series of moments that add up to a whole?

Slowly, though, I began to think that the best way to understand Smale was not as someone making specific decisions in the moment or taking actions in response to a specific problem. Rather, it was to consider Smale as someone whose gaze, even when dealing with seemingly trivial matters, was constantly fixed on the future — on what he called "the successful perpetuation of this institution."

In the late 1970s, he was planning out what P&G might need to look like in the next century. In the early 1980s, he was directing Ed Artzt to make P&G a global company. In 1985, he saw what many others didn't in the potential benefits of the purchase of Richardson-Vicks and turbocharged the company's international growth.

As CEO, he relentlessly worked to shape P&G into a company that could compete — and win — in global markets, and not just for a few years but for decades.

The more I came to understand John Smale's deep belief in the uniqueness of Procter & Gamble and the importance of preserving its culture, the more I recognized the weight of responsibility he must have carried during his years at the top of the company.

On an early trip to Cincinnati, I saw a copy of a book of his collected speeches in the company archive, titled "With All That's in Me."

I wouldn't understand what the title was referring to until speaking with Jerry Dirvin, a former executive vice president of the company. To really grasp Smale's importance to P&G, Dirvin said, it might help to study the speech Smale gave just before officially taking over as CEO.

The company was in a difficult place at that time. A few months before, Smale's predecessor, Ed Harness, had pulled Rely tampons from the market, despite serious doubts within P&G that the product was causing toxic shock syndrome. Harness was scrapping years of research, huge investments in productive capacity and what seemed certain to be years of market leadership in an important category for the company.

The Rely decision would eventually become one of the stories that P&G tells about itself — proof that the company will "do the right thing," even when it hurts. But on the night Smale spoke, the wound was still pretty raw.

It was December 1980, and the company's top executives had assembled in Cincinnati for the annual year-end management meeting. I assumed, from my conversation with Dirvin, that it had been a more subdued crowd than usual that greeted Smale when he took the podium after the meeting's closing dinner. The evening-ending speech was normally delivered by the CEO, but Harness had passed the responsibility to Smale, who would officially assume that title in three weeks.

"As I speak to you tonight for the first time, as the about-to-become chief executive officer of this company, I have many and varied emotions and feelings," he began.

"This position will be the culmination of a lifetime of association with this great company. My dominant thoughts are those of respect and humility. Respect, because this company deserves uncommon performance from those who lead it. Humility, with a clear recognition that the office is more important than the person who fills it at any given point in time."

Smale went on to express his "optimism and confidence" that P&G would continue to grow and succeed, but he warned that success could never be taken for granted. "While we are indeed blessed with a strong company, built by those who preceded us, the success of this business must be won each year, again and again. It will not continue based simply on the momentum of the past."

Dirvin had urged me to read the end of the speech closely.

"It is customary at the end of the address at these December management meetings for the speaker to wish all of you and your families a very happy holiday season and a healthy and productive new year. I'd like to do just that tonight.

"But, I'd also make a personal request of you, for your best wishes, and your prayers for me, as I assume the responsibility of the office of the chief executive officer for what has been, under the leadership of my predecessors, the greatest company in the world.

"I will try with all that's in me to see that it so remains."

Now I knew where the title of the book had come from.

Dirvin told me that the reaction to Smale's request had been electric.

"Everybody in the room got on their feet and clapped," he said. "The humility of the man ... . A lot of people stepping into that role would be trying to sell themselves, and John went the other way and said, 'I've got a tough job. This is big, and I'm going to need not only your help but your prayers.' I'll never forget that. It was a seminal moment from a standpoint of getting his leadership as the CEO off to an incredible start."

Reading that speech made it clear to me, as nothing had before, the degree to which Smale saw himself in a stewardship role at P&G. It was his job to protect and preserve the company but also to make sure that it was positioned to thrive in the years after he was gone. He needed to leave it better than he found it.

Delivering his remarks that night, he must have understood, in a way many others in the room did not, that fulfilling that purpose would require him to change the organization, both in terms of its structure and, in some ways, its culture.

————————

Tom Laco, a retired vice chairman of P&G, was particularly generous with his time as I researched some of the most fundamental changes that Smale had pushed P&G to make. The two men had become close in the late 1960s and early 1970s, usually moving in tandem through the ranks of the company, with Laco typically reporting to Smale.

By the 1980s, Smale and Laco had begun to notice how badly American firms were performing vis-à-vis their Japanese rivals. They were aware that Japanese manufacturers had adopted the "Total Quality Management" method of running their businesses, but Laco told me it wasn't until he led a team of P&G executives on a trip to visit several Japanese companies that they really understood how TQM could make a difference for P&G.

"When I came back from Japan with my team, I wrote a six-page memo, which is very unusual," Laco told me. (P&G, I knew, was famous for its insistence that the one-page memo be the standard for internal communication.)

Laco needed six pages because TQM is a complicated, sometimes counter-intuitive way of looking at business operations. The ostensible goal of TQM is nothing short of perfection. Systems and processes are to be continually refined to eliminate the possibility of error.

While there were obvious ways to apply TQM to P&G's manufacturing operations, Laco was articulating something more — a rethinking of how P&G interacted with "the trade" — companies that sold P&G products to retail consumers.

"I wrote a six-pager, and Smale got it right away. He read it and said, 'Okay, let's do that,'" Laco told me. "He stunned me. I knew he was brilliant, but the details of the concept were kind of quirky and you had to think about them a little bit. John didn't have to think about them. He got the whole thing right away."

What followed was nothing short of revolutionary for the consumer products industry. After an unsuccessful attempt to convince the Kroger grocery store chain, P&G's Cincinnati neighbor, to join it in an experiment with TQM, P&G set its sights on Walmart.

P&G executives who were working in Cincinnati at the time have a multitude of stories about P&G's relationship with Walmart, and Smale's personal relationship with its founder, Sam Walton.

As the two firms tried to rethink their relationship, there were definitely some moments when the corporate cultures clashed. P&G folks love to tell the story of how a team of Walmart executives visiting Cincinnati balked at the price of hotel rooms in the city and sent their hosts scrambling to negotiate cheaper double-occupancy rates at the Queen City Club.

The cultures may not have been a perfect fit, but the bottom line, as I came to understand it, was that John Smale cultivated and ultimately developed a close personal relationship with Walton that allowed the two firms to develop a revolutionary partnership.

In the past, P&G had sent legions of salespeople, each representing different categories of products, to call on Walmart. The negotiation over the wholesale pricing of P&G products was treated as a zero-sum game, with the companies negotiating as adversaries.

What Smale and Walton agreed to do was, instead, treat the relationship as a collaboration. P&G eventually transferred a team of executives to Arkansas, near Walmart's headquarters, and worked directly with the retailer to apply the principles of TQM to their shared goal: getting consumers to buy more P&G products from Walmart.

The result streamlined the delivery of P&G products, which enabled both companies to cut costs and improve profitability.

P&G would take a similar model to other large retailers, and within a few years, the company's competitors would be hurrying behind them, trying to create similar relationships.

Smale's decision came with significant internal disruption at P&G. The company's sales force understood that its role in the company was being significantly changed.

Tom Muccio, who led the original P&G team working with Walmart in Arkansas, told me about a presentation he gave to the managers of one of P&G's divisions after the first year of the new arrangement with Walmart. The initiative had been presented as a "pilot project," which implied that there was a possibility it would not continue.

Muccio told me that he and his team were getting a lot of pushback from the division managers, who saw some of their control slipping away. Smale entered the conference room partway through the meeting and sat through enough of the session to get a feel for the resistance Muccio was facing.

"He listened for about 40 minutes," Muccio said. "And then he stood up, and he said, 'Let's be clear. We are going to do this.'"

I tracked down part of an interview that Smale gave the company's archivist in which he described the difficulty of changing P&G's sales culture.

"The sales restructuring, of all the changes that we made, was clearly the most difficult," Smale later said. "It took longer to be accepted conceptually by the sales organizations within the divisions. ... The sales managers had serious problems, and it was a very slow process."

But Smale knew that, if P&G didn't take the lead in embracing this idea, a competitor eventually would.

"People are used to doing what they've grown up doing, but the environment had changed dramatically," he said. "Our accounts had lost interest in seeing six salesmen from six different Procter & Gamble divisions with different terms with different promotions, etc., etc. It was highly inefficient."

I thought about how much simpler it would have been for Smale to leave well enough alone. In 1988, when Smale first sent Muccio to Arkansas, P&G was doing extraordinarily well. Annual sales were up 10.6% from the previous year and were approaching $20 billion. For the first time, P&G would report annual earnings of more than $1 billion.

To the average executive at P&G, it must have seemed like a strange time to overhaul a major part of the company's operations.

But in 1988, Smale wasn't managing P&G with an eye on 1989, or even 1999. He was making sure that the institution he loved was positioned to grow well into the next century.

————

As I interviewed Smale's former colleagues, I was, again and again, told that I really needed to speak with a retired P&G executive named Dave Swanson. Swanson had been by Smale's side when he made some of his most momentous decisions about the structure of the company.

The trouble was that nobody knew how to get in touch with him. Old phone numbers were disconnected, and emails received no response.

Looking for some sort of connection, I began scouring old newspaper databases until I found a wedding announcement that appeared to be for Swanson's daughter, Jennifer. I was unable to find contact information for her, but I tracked down her husband's work email. To my delight, he responded and promised that he and his wife would call me.

Excitement quickly turned to sadness that evening. Dave Swanson, it turned out, had Alzheimer's disease and wouldn't be able to speak with me.

After expressing my sympathies, I was preparing to say goodbye when Jennifer asked me if I thought her father's book would be of any help.

"His book?" I replied. "I didn't know he had written a book."

Yes, she said. Her father had written about his life — a book that necessarily focused on his many years at P&G.

Jennifer and her husband were in Massachusetts, but her sister likely had a spare copy of the book, Jennifer said, and she lived in Maryland, less than half an hour's drive from my house in Virginia.

Early the next morning, I crossed the Potomac River into Bethesda, Maryland, and picked up a copy of *A Better Way*, by David S. Swanson. Flipping through the pages, I immediately recognized a photo of Smale. Reading more closely, I saw that Swanson had dedicated a section of the book to Smale, specifically, calling him "my Mentor-in-Chief."

The memoir recounted how, in 1987, Swanson and Smale began taking steps that would transform the way P&G's manufacturing arms operated.

Swanson was in charge of all P&G production facilities, overseeing 60 factories in the United States and 22 foreign countries. Smale, wanting to better understand the company's operations, reached out to Swanson and asked him to arrange a series of factory tours. For a full year, Swanson and Smale spent every other Wednesday traveling to the company's far-flung manufacturing facilities.

"Predictably, our technicians rose to the occasion and dazzled [Smale] with their knowledge, their insight, their humor, their pride, and their affection for the company," Swanson wrote. "In turn, John dazzled the plant people with his candor, his quickness, and his interest in them as individuals."

The trips were good for worker morale, but they also served another purpose.

Through the mid-1980s, P&G siloed responsibility for acquiring raw materials, engineering production processes, and manufacturing and delivery systems across the company. This made for an inflexible system in which decision-making was slow and innovation difficult to achieve. A change proposed at the manufacturing level would have to be sent to the engineering department and work its way to senior management there for sign-off. If the change required a different mix of raw materials, the same layered process had to take place in the purchasing division. It could take months for a helpful new idea to be implemented on the factory floor.

Swanson came to Smale with a proposal to break down the barriers in the company's supply chain by creating a position called the product supply manager, who would have authority to coordinate purchasing, engineering, manufacturing and distribution functions related to specific product areas.

It would be a tremendous change, taking responsibility away from a large number of senior executives across many divisions — but it dovetailed nicely with Smale's conviction that decision-making power at P&G needed to be pushed downward.

Though the product supply model developed independently from the switch to category management, they were implemented almost simultaneously. The effect was to place a product supply manager on the team of every new category general manager, giving the category heads the ability to expedite changes to the system.

Smale, as usual, made the change with an eye on the future.

"I have the growing conviction that the product supply concept is perhaps the single most important thing that can influence our profit performance over the next several years," Smale told *Fortune* magazine soon after the program was launched. He estimated that it would slash the company's costs by $1 billion over the coming two years — a prediction that turned out to be accurate.

———————

Before getting hold of Swanson's memoir, I already knew that he had played a key role in one of the most traumatic decisions Smale made as CEO: closing many of P&G's production facilities in the late 1980s.

The change forced P&G to reconsider an unspoken policy that had been in place since before Smale was born.

In 1923, P&G announced a policy of guaranteed employment for its workers in plants and offices across the United States — a move unprecedented at the time. At a time when other companies frequently shut factories down and sent workers home when demand flagged, P&G announced that all its workers would be guaranteed full pay for not less than 48 weeks of work per calendar year.

Over the years, employees at P&G had come to believe that a job with the company was a job for life. But that assumption was colliding with reality by the time Swanson and Smale began visiting factories in 1987.

At the same time that Smale was pushing for the adoption of Total Quality Management methods to reshape P&G's relationship with retailers, Swanson had been applying the system to manufacturing operations.

By the time Smale began visiting production facilities with Swanson, the results were clear. The combination of Total Quality Management methods in production facilities with upgraded technology had increased productivity to the point that many P&G's plants had excess personnel.

For example, P&G operated 14 different plants to produce dry laundry detergents in the mid-1980s. Within a few years, though, the company would need only three plants to produce the same amount of detergent. Similar changes played out across manufacturing operations in other business lines.

Eventually, Swanson wrote, he came to Smale with a warning: "We have reached the point where we are literally going to have to pay people for staying home."

It was clear to Smale that the company's long-standing commitment to its workforce was about to face a test.

A round of incentivized early retirements postponed the overstaffing problem for a time, but soon, productivity gains made some of P&G's older facilities redundant.

With Swanson's input, Smale gave the go-ahead to begin consolidating much of the company's sprawling manufacturing infrastructure, which inevitably led to factories being shut down.

As older plants in Long Beach, Staten Island, Chicago, and St. Louis began closing, P&G made blanket offers to workers there to relocate them and their families, at company expense, to other locations with openings.

But many wouldn't or couldn't move, and P&G, for the first time in its modern history, had to begin letting some employees go.

Swanson recalled the experience as "traumatic," both for the employees facing a loss of a job and for the managers who had to let them go.

I wondered about how Smale had felt at the time and went back to some of the videos I had received from Cathy months before. After searching the transcripts, I found a portion of a video interview in which Smale discussed the factory closings.

The sadness in his voice was obvious, even two decades later: "Those were painful experiences because, while we offered people jobs in other locations, basically most people, understandably, didn't want to move."

P&G had tried to be generous, he said, "But still and all, in a company which attaches so much importance to the relationship between employees and management and feels that their self-interests are all kind of identical, ... [it was] very painful."

However, and here was the crucial point, he added, "Clearly, it was the right thing to do for the business. ... Because the problem is, if you avoid making those decisions, because they're painful, then you end up in a worse situation, because the business suffers. And so, then suffering goes a lot deeper."

I wondered whether Smale had had that decision in mind when, a few months after the closings were announced, he drafted one of his regular columns for P&G's internal magazine, *Moonbeams*.

"A new idea or proposed change often feels uncomfortable," he wrote. "An initial reaction may be, 'This isn't the P&G way.'

"We need to challenge that thinking. While our basic values — respect for the individual, honesty and integrity — will never change, we have many practices and procedures that should change over time to meet the needs of a growing and dynamic business."

Not all of the changes that Smale pressed on P&G had to do with company structure. One of the most profound was the adoption, in the late 1980s, of a comprehensive diversity policy.

Like most American companies in the 1980s, P&G's senior management was overwhelmingly white and male. That was beginning to present a problem, not just for the image the company wished to portray, but also for its ability to compete globally.

It was a particularly pressing concern because P&G's policy of promoting from within meant that changing the racial and gender makeup of its senior management team would be a generational undertaking.

John Pepper told me that, when he had returned to Cincinnati in the late 1970s, after working in P&G's European operations for several years, he brought back with him the conviction that the company needed to be more aggressive about pursuing a diverse workforce.

A decade later, while overseeing North American operations as president of the company, Pepper began taking steps to make P&G's employee base more representative of the consumers it served. He told me that he had assumed that he would find, in Smale, a willing partner.

I would have thought so, too. After all, Smale was the former chairman of the United Negro College Fund. In 1982, residents of Cincinnati would have seen him on their televisions in a public service announcement, urging people to donate to the UNCF's annual fundraising campaign.

In 1985, Smale had told an audience at Saint Augustine's College, a historically black institution in North Carolina, "This society ... will not, in fact, fulfill its real promise until we have created a society of true equal opportunity."

But when Pepper first came to Smale with the idea of creating a task force to hammer out an official diversity policy, he found the CEO oddly cautious. He would send a memo to Smale recommending the task force's creation, only to have it come back with requests for a better definition of the business purpose.

"I know John felt, for a period of time, that I kind of had my head in the clouds," Pepper told me. "He wouldn't have said it that way, but I get carried away, and I can remember presenting a plan for the U.S., and he said, 'John, what's the business case for this? I believe you're doing the right thing,' he said, 'but you have not presented a compelling business case.'"

Pepper said he bristled at that, believing he had presented a very clear case. Besides, he thought, it was obviously the right thing to do.

As with the statement of Purpose, Values, & Principles, though, Smale's initial instinct was to tread carefully.

Pepper took the initiative and launched a diversity program across P&G's North American operations. He assembled a Diversity Task Force, including Ed Artzt and Tom Laco, and, on a Friday in January 1989, asked Smale to attend a meeting of that group. The following Monday, Pepper, Artzt and Laco all received a densely written two-page memo from Smale.

"It seems to me to be very important that the four of us get our minds around this subject and how we think the company ought to approach it before the 'Diversity Task Force' gets much further along," Smale began.

It was an inauspicious start, Pepper thought.

Reading further, though, he began to realize that Smale's concerns weren't precisely what he had imagined them to be. All along, the CEO's critiques had been about mushy language, and this memo was no exception. "The language surrounding these discussions is full of jargon," Smale wrote.

"If what we're talking about importantly relates to the need to bring black men and women and white women into higher positions of responsibility in the company, and if in order to do that, we've concluded that we have to make changes in our way of dealing with these groups, then we, I think, ought to come out and say it just that simply."

But what really seized Pepper's attention was a different section:

"It seems to me that we are dealing here with a core value of the company," Smale wrote. "While in principle it is not a new value, we are discussing and making it a major specific 'project' throughout the company. It will be a multi-year project that will require a great deal of time and attention on the part of the managers throughout the company. It's important, then, at the outset, that we recognize that this is not a U.S. operating business issue, but one of company-wide — both line and staff — significance."

Pepper told me he realized then that Smale had been taking a much broader view of the diversity effort, looking at it not just as something to apply in the United States but globally. The language in the policy would have to be precise and applicable not just in Cincinnati but also in Egypt, India, Venezuela and the dozens of other countries where P&G did business.

This didn't make birthing a company diversity policy any easier, and the back and forth over language sometimes irritated both Pepper and Smale.

The CEO urged the task force to be less "preachy" in its writing: "I have a real problem going to our organization and sounding as if we were approaching them from some moral high ground. I would find this objectionable myself as an employee because I think it tends to be presumptuous and sees the management talking down to our fellow employees about a subject that we have no right to talk down about."

After a year of back-and-forth discussion, P&G finalized a comprehensive diversity strategy that would eventually be rolled out globally. Goals were baked into the compensation schemes of managers, and the company initiated a campaign to identify and recruit top young talent from the same historically black colleges and universities that Smale had long supported through his work with the United Negro College Fund.

Crucially, Smale transformed from a tentative supporter of the policy to its chief champion.

Once he was sure that the policy was, in Pepper's words, "well founded," Smale understood that to properly implement it across the organization, the strategy had to come directly from the CEO.

"He really took it out there," Pepper recalled. "In many cases, bravely, and got it in front of the organization as only a CEO could."

Over the ensuing decades, P&G would aggressively pursue greater diversity in the company, compiling awards for its efforts and creating a pipeline of talent into senior management.

The corporation John Smale took over in January 1980 would be vastly changed by the end of that decade. Smale had revitalized the company's research and development operation, tapping into a stream of innovative new products that would continue for years after his departure.

The company's old divisional structure had been jettisoned in favor of a more streamlined category system that produced stunning results, such as turning the struggling Pringles brand into a billion-dollar behemoth.

Smale had overhauled both P&G's sales operations and its production arm, creating synergies between the company and its retail partners and, at the same time, driving down costs. Competitors would struggle for years to match P&G in either aspect of their businesses.

He had backed the creation of the company's statement of Purpose, Values, & Principles, which is still in place today, as well as a diversity policy that helped P&G consistently rank as one of corporate America's best places to work.

When Smale announced his retirement in late 1989, he could be secure in the belief that the company was as well prepared for the future as he could possibly have made it.

He went out on as high a note as possible, too: For the fiscal year ending in June 1989, P&G profits had hit an all-time high of $1.2 billion, more than double the company's earnings in the year prior to Smale taking over as CEO. In October, barely one-quarter of the way through the new fiscal year, analysts were predicting another 20% jump in annual earnings.

The stock market had also taken notice. A year previously, the value of a share of P&G stock had been hovering in the range of $80 to $90. On the day Smale announced his retirement, it was trading at just shy of $131 per share. In fact, the growth had been so sharp that one order of business at that year's annual meeting was a vote on a 2-for-1 stock split, a move designed to make investing in P&G more affordable for average investors by cutting the stock price in half while doubling the number of shares in circulation.

Smale spoke to managers at the year-end meeting in 1989, just before he handed the reins to Ed Artzt. Of all the hours of video of Smale that I have seen, it's the only time he ever comes even close to losing his composure.

In his brief remarks to the thousands of assembled P&G employees, Smale plainly struggled to hold his emotions in check. He cited no numbers, listed no accomplishments and remained on the stage for a little less than five minutes.

He reminded the crowd of the speech he had delivered nine years earlier, as he prepared to take over as CEO. At the time, he recalled, he had asked them for their prayers.

"There have been many times during these past nine years when, in the dark hours of night, I've yearned for more insight, and for better answers than I felt I had to the problems that the business faced," he said. "But never — never once — did I doubt that I indeed did have your best wishes and that I had your prayers. It has been a high honor to have had the opportunity to be the chief executive of this company. The successes that we've had are yours. They're due to you. Everything that's been accomplished has been achieved by all of us, working together, and that's why this is indeed the greatest company in the world. Because you make it so. God bless you. God bless this company."

With that, as the crowd erupted into a standing ovation, John Smale shook Artzt's hand and stepped through a gap in the curtain, leaving the stage at P&G.

Watching that video, as I have a number of times, I try to force myself to take it in as a member of the audience might have — a witness to the end of an astounding career.

The trouble is that I know something nobody in that room could have. I know that Smale was stepping off one stage, only to be called almost immediately onto another — one that would make him a household name not just in Cincinnati but in much of the United States.

CHAPTER 17

General Motors: The Obligation to Act

Any journalist can tell you that there are plenty of ways to screw up an interview. You can turn up unprepared. You can lead with a question that your subject considers unnecessarily hostile. You can let yourself be charmed and forget to press your subject on the one issue you really should have explored in depth. You can act as though you understand a subject you don't and miss the opportunity to actually learn something.

In more than 25 years in the business, across thousands of interviews, I've been guilty of some version of each of these on occasion.

But I have never, ever, screwed up an interview as spectacularly as when I went to visit Ira Millstein, the legendary attorney and advisor to public company boards of directors across the United States.

I needed to speak with Millstein in order to tell the story of how John Smale oversaw the turnaround of General Motors in the 1990s. As a member of the board of directors, Smale had wrested partial control of the board from the company's domineering CEO, Roger Smith, whose vision was to turn the storied carmaker into a financial-services conglomerate with a sideline in automobiles.

Under Smale's leadership, the independent members of the board of directors began meeting separately from GM management — something unheard of at the time — and banded together to begin forcing change on the company.

Then, when Smith's successor refused to implement the broad-based reforms that the board believed were necessary, Smale oversaw his ouster and the replacement of his entire management team, becoming chairman of the board himself.

The changes Smale wrought at GM reverberated through the business world, igniting new interest in the idea that ensuring good "corporate governance" was the affirmative duty of directors of a public company. And many CEOs who resisted the change found themselves suddenly out of a job.

Millstein, in private practice with the New York firm Weil, Gotshal & Manges, was the attorney advising the independent directors during Smale's time with the automaker. It had been Millstein, in concert with GM's general counsel, Harry Pearce, who had convinced Smale and his fellow board members of the need to take radical action to save the company.

Nobody was better placed to help me understand John Smale's time at GM, and I was grateful that he had agreed to see me. Millstein was, at the time, 92 years old. My impression, from speaking with Sally Sasso, his longtime assistant, was that he scheduled about one event per day. I felt lucky to be on his calendar.

I was to meet Millstein in Mamaroneck, N.Y., a short train ride north of Manhattan, where he lived in a house with a stunning view across Long Island Sound.

To prepare for the interview, I had read Millstein's book, *The Activist Director,* about how, in the 1990s, corporate boards had awakened to their responsibility to rein in management. I had read other accounts of the turnaround of GM in which Millstein figured prominently, including *Comeback,* by the *Wall Street Journal's* Pulitzer Prize-winning team of veteran automotive correspondents, Paul Ingrassia and Joseph B. White, whose account deeply informs this chapter.

I had pored over transcripts of Smale's interviews with GM's archivists and read his various speeches to the company's management team. As my taxi pulled up to the gate restricting access to Millstein's neighborhood, I felt as ready for the interview as I could possibly be.

But I was a week early.

I had arranged the interview through Sasso. We had gone back and forth a few times on possible dates, and during a phone conversation with her, I had typed what I thought was the final date for our meeting into my calendar. When she followed up shortly thereafter with a confirming email, I barely glanced at it.

As instructed, I called Sasso from the cab when I was on the way from the train station. She was beside herself when she learned I was just about to go knock on her boss's door a full seven days before he was expecting me. It took me about 30 seconds and a quick scroll on my phone, back to that unread email, to realize my mistake.

Sasso told me that Millstein had already participated in one conference call that morning and wasn't supposed to tire himself any further. But she said I should wait while she called him.

I sent the cab on its way while I waited for her to call me back, thinking that I might as well walk the two miles back to the train station and give myself time to really appreciate the monumental quality of this disaster.

My phone rang, and it was Sasso. Millstein would still see me, she said.

I would genuinely have preferred to slink back to the train station and disappear from Mamaroneck forever, but I threw my bag over my shoulder, and trudged grimly down the road toward Millstein's house.

An aide met me at the door and, with all the side-eye I deserved, told me to wait in the foyer while she let Millstein know I had arrived. A few minutes later, she led me upstairs, into his office.

Behind his desk, Millstein sat bolt-upright. His head was framed by a halo of white curly hair, and he wore pajamas and a dressing gown, which he somehow managed to make look more formal than my jacket and open-collared shirt.

Also, he was furious.

I hadn't even had a chance to sit down before he opened fire. "This is your foul-up! I don't have to talk to you," he said.

I agreed. It was, indeed, my foul-up, I said. I offered my unconditional apologies to him and to Sasso, who wasn't in the house but was working from the law firm's offices in Manhattan. I offered to leave, hoping to do as little damage as possible to my chance to speak with him at a different time in the future.

But Millstein wasn't done with me. He demanded to know how I could possibly have gotten the date wrong. Sasso had sent him our email chain. It was as clear as day that I was supposed to be there next week.

Again, I agreed. I had no defense. I could only repeat my apologies and an offer to leave him in peace. We went back and forth like this for several minutes. A couple of times, I thought I felt him soften his tone, only to hear the anger rise again.

After a while, I began to get angry, too. I had certainly made a colossal mess of things, but I had also apologized, humbly and in good faith. I found my answers to Millstein becoming clipped and harsh, and I considered simply walking out of the house.

But then he said something that brought me up short.

"I'm 92 years old," he said. "You didn't give me time to prepare."

The sudden clarity hit me like a slap in the face. Yes, Millstein was mad at me for screwing up the schedule. But the real issue here — the reason why I felt him vacillating between starting a conversation and throwing me out — was that I had created a situation in which he was afraid he wouldn't be able to do justice to John Smale.

That was my real foul-up.

Subtly, the tone of the conversation began to shift. I mentioned to Millstein that I had read his book and was very interested in everything he and Smale had done at GM, and how they had gone on to revolutionize the concept of corporate governance in the United States.

Still, I was sure the best possible outcome from the visit would be obtaining an agreement to get together again in the future, when Millstein had had time to prepare. After a few minutes, I floated the idea again.

"I suspect that's the best thing to do," he said, not unkindly.

"If I have had an opportunity to look over my history, we can reconvene on the phone. Now that you've seen the body," he said, gesturing to himself, "I don't think you need necessarily to do it again."

I agreed and was gathering my things when Millstein started talking again. Did I want to understand why he was so concerned about doing Smale justice, he asked.

I said I did.

He pointed to a shelf full of pictures and counted off: "One, two, three ... four. Fourth from the right."

I picked it up and saw a picture of Millstein and Smale, standing together near what appeared to be a newly planted sapling.

"What's the significance of the tree?" I asked.

"It was for his wife, Phyllis," Millstein said. I looked again at the photo. Smale looked older in it than he had during his GM days. I assumed it must have been taken some time after Phyllis's death in 2006.

I asked Millstein if it had been taken in Cincinnati, thinking it had likely been one of the many garden spots Smale had dedicated to his wife in the city where they had spent almost their entire married life.

"No," he said. "That's Central Park."

I didn't know much about the rules for adding trees to Central Park, but I did know that the oasis in the heart of Manhattan was one of the most closely monitored and managed public green spaces in the world. You couldn't just show up with a shovel and start planting things.

I also knew that Millstein had served as chairman of the Central Park Conservancy and later as the chair of the Central Park Conservancy Institute for Urban Parks.

"He wanted to plant a tree in honor of Phyllis," Millstein said. "We don't generally let people do that. And there's a plaque there, which we don't ordinarily do for people, either. But this was John."

Smale had asked to plant a tree dedicated to his wife, with a plaque memorializing her, in a park more than 500 miles away from the city where she had spent the bulk of her life.

Millstein had made it happen.

"Obviously, you can see the degree of esteem in which I held him," he said.

He continued, "The thing about John was everybody trusted him. Everybody. And you can't say any more than that. That's before he became chairman. If there was an issue [before the board] which people wanted to think about, all heads turned to John to see what he thought.

"And that trust was earned. Because whatever he did was transparent. Good for the company. Not self-aggrandizement. He didn't want [to do] any of the things that, ultimately, he had to do. But there was nobody else to do it."

I mentioned that, in the end, what Smale and Millstein had done had been good not just for GM but also for corporate America writ large.

"We had no idea that we were making history," he said. "Nor did we intend to make history. We intended to change General Motors. And we did."

I had a hard time believing that. Hadn't they had practically invented a new paradigm for the management of public companies?

"What did we invent?" Millstein asked. "We invented the right thing to do."

I smiled at the not-so-faint echo of the P&G mantra and took my leave of Millstein, glad to have salvaged something from the day and grateful that I'd get the chance to speak with him again.

————

From my research, I knew that Smale had always been a "car guy." Early in his career at P&G, he would sometimes drag Phyllis to weekend car shows, where he would stare at vehicles he couldn't possibly afford. But when P&G named him president of the company in 1974, he decided that his handsome salary of $325,000 per year gave him the ability to do more than just look. Working through a specialized car importer, he bought himself a Jensen Interceptor Mark III. With a monstrous eight-cylinder, 440-cubic-inch Chrysler engine, the Interceptor was capable of cruising comfortably at 125 miles per hour.

Smale was aware that the car stood out sharply when he pulled it into his reserved parking spot in the company garage, but he felt he had earned what he would later call his "moment of hubris."

Peter Smale, the youngest of the Smales' four children, told me that he had never forgotten the time, when he was about 13 years old, his father had taken the Jensen up to 110 miles per hour on an empty stretch of Canadian highway, just enjoying the sheer power of the car. Neither Smale nor Peter ever mentioned that adventure to Phyllis.

The Jensen was something of a lesson in cars for Smale. While he loved it, it also frustrated him. The sports car's brilliant handling and sleek looks were offset by constant electrical failures and other problems. He would sometimes complain that owning a Jensen meant that you had to buy a second car, so that you had something to drive when the Interceptor was in the shop.

It was the sort of thing that drove someone brought up in the culture of P&G a little crazy. If one out of every 10 tubes of Crest toothpaste was defective, it wouldn't matter how good the dentifrice inside was. Customers would stop buying it.

After a few years, Smale sold the Jensen, but the interest in cars never faded, so in 1982, when he had the opportunity to join the board of General Motors, he took it.

What Smale couldn't have known at the time was that GM, the largest automaker in the United States and one of the largest employers in the world, was entering a prolonged state of decline. In 1980, nearly half of all the cars sold in the United States were manufactured by GM, but cheaper, well-made Japanese imports were chipping away at that market share.

Along with the tougher competition, GM was plagued by labor disputes, manufacturing inefficiencies and a marked decline in the quality and variety of the vehicles it was producing. By the mid-1980s, GM had been surpassed in manufacturing efficiency not just by the Japanese but also by its major U.S. competitors, Ford and Chrysler. The company had fallen behind on innovation, as well. The engines in GM's vehicles had hardly changed in decades.

When Smale joined the GM board, though, much of this information was unavailable to the non-employee board members, known as "outside directors." Chief Executive Officer Roger Smith ruled the company with tyrannical authority. When challenged, he would fly into towering rages that became legendary among subordinates and board members alike.

In Smith's board meetings, outside directors were spoon-fed very general information, often sitting across the table from inside directors supplied with far more detailed board books. Many of the most important decisions were restricted to the board's finance committee, made up of Smith's closest supporters.

The more I read about the way GM was managed in the 1980s, the more shocking I found it. But Harry Pearce, who took over in 1987 as the company's general counsel, told me it wasn't seen as remarkable at all.

"In many respects it was pretty typical of how boards operated in major companies in the U.S.," Pearce said. "They tended to be sort of men's clubs. They all knew one another. And they viewed it as an honor to be on the board of a large company. Most of them were CEOs of their own substantial companies, and it was not the kind of environment that evoked careful review of business decisions that the board may have felt were inappropriate."

That tracked with something Smale had said, with some evident regret, when he spoke with GM's archivists years later.

"I think, in earlier days, it was much more of an [honor] to be asked to go on a board," Smale said. "And people used to go on several. It was not unusual for a chief executive officer to be on his own board, plus maybe four or five others."

The meetings were short, and the commitment didn't demand much from board members, he'd said.

It occurred to me that my career as a business reporter had begun in the late 1990s. The reason why GM's management in the 1980s seemed so strange was that I had grown up as a journalist in a world significantly transformed by what Smale would do at General Motors.

———————

Even before GM's financial woes began to become apparent in the late 1980s, Smale started to question the way the company was being run. He would often come back to Cincinnati after trips to Detroit and bounce things off of P&G executives like Ed Artzt.

Artzt told me about several conversations with Smale during his time at GM.

As a director, Smale was frequently brought in to observe new products and production methods. It was a task he generally enjoyed, just as he had loved new product reviews during his years at P&G. On one trip to Detroit, he told Artzt, he was given the chance to look at a soon-to-be-released new model of one of GM's existing cars. After the development engineers finished with their demonstration of the car, Smale asked if he could take a closer look. He pulled open one of the doors, noticing as he did that it was remarkably heavy.

Sitting down in the car with the door closed, he inspected the interior, and then moved to get back out again. But from the low angle of the seat, even Smale — not a small man — had to strain to push the heavy door open again.

"I don't think the average woman is going to have an easy time getting out of this car," he told the engineers. "Have you done any consumer research on the new door configuration?"

The engineers shook their heads. One of them looked at Smale and said, "Why would we do that? The consumer doesn't know shit about the car business."

To Smale and Artzt, that attitude was stunning. At P&G, market-testing new products and changes to existing products was an article of faith. It was ingrained in everyone that the consumer was the boss, and the consumer's preferences should be the starting point for any change or addition to a product.

Smale told Artzt, "I couldn't believe what I was hearing. But that's the GM mentality: If you're not in the car business, what do you know?"

Another time, in the mid-'80s, Smale called up Artzt and offered to give him a ride in a new concept car that he was test-driving between board meetings.

Within GM's research arm, engineers had cobbled together an all-electric car — a novelty at the time. Artzt was charmed by the odd little vehicle that, seemingly by magic, whisked the two of them around town, making barely any noise at all.

"Would you believe these guys don't have a plan for marketing this thing?" Smale said. "They just developed it and here it is. Now I'm driving around Cincinnati in it, but there aren't going to be any for sale. They're not planning to make any. I don't know what the hell they're thinking."

That was, in fact, part of the problem. Smale, as he would later come to realize, really ought to have known what GM's management was thinking. That he and the other board members didn't was becoming a major concern for Ira Millstein and Harry Pearce.

———

By the late 1980s, GM's market share was in free fall, and its North American operation, the company's largest, was suffering the most. Huge factories were going unused, and GM's cost per vehicle manufactured was a full $1,000 over the costs of its rival, Ford.

Pearce and Millstein were worried that the management of GM wasn't getting the benefit of the wisdom and experience of a board stacked with giant figures in corporate America. In addition to Smale, board members from the business world included Jim Evans, the former chairman of Union Pacific; Bill Marriott, CEO of his family's hotel chain; Ed Pratt, the chairman of the drug company Pfizer; Tom Wyman, the former CEO and chairman of CBS; and Dennis Weatherstone, the president and later CEO of J.P. Morgan & Co.

But Pearce and Millstein were also worried about something else: the threat of shareholder lawsuits against the outside board members if the extent of GM's troubles became public. This threat weighed particularly on Millstein, as outside counsel to the board's independent directors. While rare, it was not unheard of for shareholders to take a company's directors to court if they believed major problems with the business were allowed to develop because the board failed to exercise sufficient oversight.

The two attorneys warned Smith that, because directors were not being given the full picture of GM's business struggles, they might not be protected from lawsuits under rules that gave them safe harbor so long as they executed their roles faithfully and made decisions based on their best business judgment.

They reminded him that major decisions had been taken by GM management with little or no input from the board of directors. For example, the minutes of board meetings would show that the directors had barely debated an expensive restructuring of the company. If the restructuring had successfully turned the North American vehicle operations around, there wouldn't have been an issue. But it hadn't. It had failed miserably.

Pearce and Millstein recommended steps that Smith could take to change the relationship between the board and GM's management, including the provision of more relevant information to board members. He could also encourage them to be more aggressive about questioning management's decisions.

Smith could take these steps himself, they said, or run the risk that the outside directors got concerned enough to become active on their own.

In fact, Smale and the other outside directors had become increasingly concerned about the condition of the company. By the end of 1988, the good-news-only board briefings had become impossible to square with Wall Street's dubious view of GM's future and the constant stream of media accounts exposing the poor quality of its cars.

Smale reached out to Smith personally more than once, asking that the board get more information about North American operations and details about Smith's promises of a turnaround that would be completed by 1992 — two years after the CEO was scheduled to retire.

Smale's oldest son, Jay, told me that his father had come to feel a sense of personal responsibility for GM's plight. Some of Smith's most disastrous decisions had occurred on his watch. They had often happened without his knowledge, or at least without his full understanding of the facts. But in the end, that was a weak excuse. As a member of the board, he was entitled to virtually any information about the company that he wanted. But he had failed to demand it.

"He felt he had to act," Jay told me. "He was obligated to act."

———————

That obligation was hammered home by Millstein who, by 1988, had begun counseling Smale and others to be more assertive with GM management.

In April, Smale sent a letter to Chief Financial Officer Alan Smith, demanding "a more detailed understanding of the [projected] genesis of the turn-around in the North American profit" and an opportunity to "look at the building blocks on the North American operations that produced the estimate for 1992 versus the current year."

He had reason to hope that the CFO would be more forthcoming than other GM executives, because Alan Smith was one of the few senior people in the company ringing alarm bells about financial performance.

His answer to Smale, though, left only more questions. And by June, the CEO had grown tired of Alan Smith's habit of reporting bad financial news. He had moved him to another position and replaced him with Robert O'Connell, a Roger Smith protégé whose go-to joke, when asked about the next quarter's profits, was that they would be "whatever you want me to make them."

In June, Smale sent another note to management, titled, "Changes in the procedure and conceptual approach relating to the General Motors board and outside directors."

The following month, Smale wrote to Roger Smith directly, complaining that the board was not spending sufficient time addressing important issues, such as the company's declining market share, and that its committee structure was ill-suited to its actual needs.

Smale wasn't the only outside director pestering Smith. Millstein's warning had an effect on others, as well. Marvin L. "Murph" Goldberger, the brilliant theoretical physicist who was then running the Institute for Advanced Study in Princeton, N.J., was firing off his own letters, as were Bill Marriott and Jim Evans.

The response from GM's CEO was pure passive-aggression. The board members wanted more information, so he arranged to make the board books — documents provided in advance of board meetings — enormous. They became, Smale would later recall, "unbelievably large," stuffed with redundant documents and endless spreadsheets, all designed to obscure the board's view of the company, not to enhance it.

On Dec. 14, 1989, GM's outside directors woke to the kind of headline in the *Wall Street Journal* that nobody in charge of a public company wants to read: "With Its Market Share Sliding, GM Scrambles to Avoid a Calamity."

The story by Paul Ingrassia and Joseph B. White was a devastating and detailed takedown of GM in the Roger Smith era. They documented the company's plummeting U.S. market share, which had just hit a 60-year low, its history of building poor-quality vehicles, and its disastrous attempts to compete with Japanese carmakers, especially in the market for mid-sized, moderately priced family cars, once the company's bread and butter.

Most alarming to the company's outside directors was the reporters' assessment of their performance during Smith's tenure. With his retirement pending in August of 1990, Smith was closing in on nine years at the head of the company.

"Many wonder how he has managed to stay so long, despite the accelerating erosion of GM's position," they wrote.

"Several outside directors, reached by telephone last week, declined to discuss the matter. But GM's directors — whose names are engraved on brass plates attached to their tall leather chairs in its New York board room — obviously hate to make waves."

The article described the outside directors, in particular, as a "cross-section of the establishment" and went on to name a handful — Smale first among them. "A tradition of clubby comfort prevails in the GM board room," they added. "Each outside director gets a new GM car of his or her choice every three months."

For Smale and the other outside directors, Millstein's warnings were beginning to look alarmingly prescient.

———————

At the time, the idea of outside directors meeting alone — especially to discuss the CEO — was completely foreign to corporate America. CEOs, who very often served as board chairs, tended to jealously guard their ability to control the meetings of directors. Nowhere was that more true than at General Motors under Roger Smith.

One day in the mid-1980s, for example, Millstein was invited to lunch by Ellmore Patterson, a GM board member who was also the former chairman and CEO of J.P. Morgan. Patterson wanted to discuss the raging fiscal crisis in New York City, where he and Millstein both lived and worked. They passed an uneventful lunch at the Plaza Hotel, across the street from the GM building in Manhattan, where Millstein had an office.

Millstein had been back in his office for only a few moments when his door flew open and Roger Smith burst inside, demanding to know what Millstein had discussed during his "unauthorized" meeting with Patterson.

Millstein answered honestly, telling Smith that the conversation had nothing to do with General Motors. However, he added, there was no such thing as an unauthorized meeting between one of the outside directors of GM and the attorney they had hired to represent them.

"I'm counsel to the board, and I can meet with a director if he or she asks," Millstein said.

Red-faced and angry, Smith barked back, "No, you can't! You're not to meet with my directors alone!" and stormed out of the office.

So, it was with a certain amount of trepidation that the outside board members of GM concluded, in early 1990, that they needed to begin meeting privately, especially to discuss choosing a successor for Smith, who was due to retire in August.

Millstein was the driving force behind the meeting. He told me how he had convened the outside directors on a conference call to finalize the plans. The preparations had been so secret that nothing had been written down or circulated through the usual channels at GM.

The secrecy bothered Smale, a former chairman and CEO himself. As convinced as he was of the severity of GM's problems and the need to rein in Roger Smith, something felt wrong about secret meetings and furtive communications. If he'd had his way, the outside directors would simply have informed Smith of their plan to meet alone and let him blow his top, if he chose to.

But others on the board were less willing to confront Smith directly and had to be eased into the idea of cutting him out of the loop.

On the call, Millstein told the outside directors that he had reserved a conference room at the Ritz-Carlton Hotel in Dearborn, a suburb of Detroit where the outside directors usually stayed. The night before the next board meeting, he said, they could all assemble there, far from GM's corporate offices, and have a candid discussion about their next move.

When the time came, it was plain that, like Smale, many of the outside directors were there reluctantly. Some, including Ed Pratt, the chairman of Pfizer, were uncomfortable with the idea of the outside directors going behind the CEO's back. Others, like Murph Goldberger, were nervous about the fallout. Smith had been terrorizing the GM board for so long, it wasn't clear what would happen if he learned about the meeting.

The meeting began awkwardly, with some of the directors still nervous that Smith might find out what they were doing.

"So what?" Millstein argued. "You're *directors*. You are, by law, in charge of the corporation."

The board members were still speaking among themselves when, suddenly, the door opened. Into the room strode a visibly agitated Roger Smith. Somehow, he had found out not only that the directors were meeting alone, but precisely where.

"This looks like a directors meeting," he said, moving across the room to take a chair. "I'd like to join you."

It was a make-or-break moment for the outside directors of General Motors. If they allowed Smith to take over this meeting, they could essentially give up on the possibility of ever standing up to him in the future.

Though he hadn't convened the meeting and felt conflicted about its circumstances, it was Smale who grasped the gravity of the situation: Now that Smith knew the outside directors were working together independently, he would view them as hostile, whether they allowed him to remain in the meeting or not.

The only way out was through.

According to Millstein, Smale stood up, faced the furious CEO and said, "This is a meeting of *outside* directors. We want to meet without you, Roger."

Smith was plainly incensed. "You can't do that!" he declared angrily.

Smale was unmoved. "Yes, we can," he said. "You're excused."

The room went silent for a moment as the two men faced each other, Smale grim-faced but calm, Smith boiling with rage. Then Smith turned on his heel and walked out of the room, slamming the door shut behind him.

Millstein told me that the outside directors' decision to stand up to Roger Smith and exercise their right to meet independently was a landmark moment for corporate America.

"That was monumental," he said. "It was considered traitorous. It just wasn't done."

But like the little stone that starts an avalanche, the effects weren't visible immediately.

Throughout early 1990, the board continued to bend to Smith's will on significant matters. It's difficult to understand exactly why the board, now clearly at odds with the CEO, continued to defer to him. Even Smale's papers shed little light on it.

The explanation that, to me, makes the most sense is that the board members, many of them current or former CEOs themselves, simply felt conflicted about appearing to take control of the company, despite Millstein's frequent reminders that, under the law, the CEO served at their pleasure.

Smith's dominance was most obvious in the selection of his successor. Despite Millstein's continued reminders that it was the board's decision, and the board's decision alone, who the next CEO of General Motors would be, Roger Smith successfully pressed them to appoint one of his most loyal subordinates, Bob Stempel.

A brilliant automotive engineer and a lifetime GM employee, Stempel was nonetheless little known to the board. The outside members agreed to support him as Smith's replacement, but not before making it clear to Stempel that they expected a very different relationship than they had had with Smith. As Goldberger put it at the time, "it must be made unambiguously clear that we have no intention of being terrorized as in the past."

Some worried that Smith, who would remain on the GM board after stepping down, would have outsize influence over Stempel. But this was outweighed by the hope that placing a "car guy" at the head of GM, rather than someone who rose through the finance department, would result in more focus on the quality issues that were harming the company in the marketplace.

In his early days as CEO, Stempel seemed prepared to do exactly what the board had hoped. In September, he negotiated a new contract with the United Auto Workers labor union and ordered a $2.1 billion write-off to pay for the closing of seven U.S.-based car factories and a number of other facilities.

In early 1991, Stempel even went so far as cutting the GM shareholder dividend nearly in half and announcing sweeping staff reductions over the coming two years.

Had he continued in that vein, things might have been different, but Stempel plainly felt that he had done enough and began counseling the board to be patient, insisting that the company would soon turn around.

The company did not, however, and Smale and other board members began reaching out to Stempel that spring, in letters and personal meetings, urging more aggressive action to avert the crisis they believed was coming.

Throughout 1991, though, Stempel remained convinced that all that was needed was more time.

In November, his calls for patience lost all potency. Standard & Poor's, which rates the creditworthiness of large companies, placed General Motors on "credit watch with negative implications." That meant there was significant danger the company would lose the ability to get favorable interest rates on its debt.

"Earnings performance by GM has been far worse than was assumed by S&P in February," the company wrote, and "losses in North America have reached unprecedented levels." S&P predicted that "wrenching new cost-cutting initiatives" would be necessary.

The announcement set off alarms both inside and outside the company. General counsel Harry Pearce, still doing his best to light a fire under the independent directors, sent a copy of the S&P report to them with a cover letter warning that GM's credit rating could face a significant downgrade in early 1992.

"Should that occur, there is a very real risk that GM's historic financial strength could unravel rather quickly," Pearce wrote. "I hope that I am being unduly pessimistic about this, but I suspect that's not the case. My best judgment is that I'm simply being realistic."

At the next board meeting, in December, Stempel stunned the directors by proposing no changes in response to the S&P report. When the board meeting ended without the announcement of a plan to get the company's financial situation in order, the stock market reacted violently. GM's shares dropped to a four-year low, cutting the value of investors' holdings by $825 million.

Even before that meeting, board members had begun losing faith in Stempel. Some had even circulated a draft statement, written in Stempel's name, announcing that he would step down from his position as chairman and allow the board to elect a new leader.

A group of outside directors headed by Tom Wyman, the former chairman of CBS, began pressing Smale to step into a role he did not relish. They wanted him to undertake a "fact-finding mission" within GM, gathering all the information he could on the company's condition and interviewing key executives in private to decide how best to move forward.

Smale was concerned that it might appear he was undermining Stempel. At the same time, he recognized that GM was approaching a crisis from which it might not be able to recover. So, he said he would agree to the task only if there was absolute unanimity among the outside directors that it was necessary.

In early January 1992, the outside directors unanimously approved a statement that Smale had been designated "to develop such information as may be necessary and desirable to further enable those directors to fulfill their responsibilities diligently and prudently during this period of difficulty for the Corporation."

The statement made it clear that the board expected complete cooperation from Stempel and the GM executive team, including access to financial and quality data. Smale also supplied a draft memo that the board required Stempel to send out in his own name, directing executives contacted by Smale to provide candid answers to his questions.

From late January through early March, Smale and a small team burrowed deeply into GM's financial position and sat down for extensive interviews with at least 20 senior executives.

Smale had his findings placed in bright red binders, perhaps to illustrate the severity of his conclusions.

Among other things, Smale had determined that out of dozens of individual car models sold across the GM family in 1990 and 1991, the company had lost money on all but two. It cost GM $530 more than Ford to produce the average vehicle coming off the assembly lines. Compared to its Japanese competitors, GM's costs were between $860 and $1,130 more per vehicle.

Smale found that GM management also knew that, as an organization, GM was vastly overstaffed, with salaried head count between 30% and 40% larger than Ford.

Finally, internal projections suggested that the company's largest division, North American Automobile Operations, was on track to lose $22 billion over the seven years ending in 1992.

None of that information had been shared with the board of directors.

Smale's interviews with GM executives were, if possible, even more alarming. Most regarded Stempel's recent prediction that the North American business would return to break-even status by 1994 as unlikely at best and ridiculous at worst. Others spoke of bankruptcy as a very real concern.

George E. Golden, GM's treasurer, told Smale, "I see the deterioration of our financial situation every day around me." Asked about the possibility of GM being forced into bankruptcy, he said, "We're not on the brink, but we're closer than ever before, and our position is eroding rapidly."

Smale described part of his conversation with George Eads, the company's vice president for product planning and economic staff:

> I began the conversation, as I have with all of the interviewees, by saying that I didn't plan to repeat any of their comments to GM management. He responded by saying, "I've reached a point where

I don't care if you tell management what I say or not. If things don't get better here in about three months, I'm going to be gone." He went on to say, "A lot of us have been wondering how long it would take the Board to begin the process that you're apparently in now."

After Smale presented his findings, the outside directors decided that a shake-up of senior management was necessary, including the firing of GM's president, chief financial officer, vice chairman of the board and executive vice president for corporate staff.

The jury remained out on Stempel. Smale and others believed they owed the CEO of General Motors a chance to explain himself, so they decided to hold another meeting the following Saturday and invited Stempel to appear.

On a personal level, John Smale had always liked Bob Stempel. In memos and letters, he repeatedly expressed his admiration for Stempel's depth of knowledge about the process of designing and building cars, and he viewed him as an honest and genuinely decent person. He also recognized that Stempel was facing some extraordinary challenges, not all of which came from inside General Motors. He had been CEO for precisely one day before the Gulf War started in 1990, triggering an oil-price shock and an economic recession, both of which hit the company hard.

But Smale also had more insight into Stempel's management style than did other members of the board of directors, because of a key connection on the inside. GM's chief economist, Marina von Neumann Whitman, was also a member of Procter & Gamble's board of directors, creating an informal back channel that helped Smale understand the workings of the company.

In a conversation with me, Whitman jokingly referred to herself as GM's "Cassandra," because she was able to accurately predict coming disasters but was doomed to be ignored.

From Whitman, Smale learned that Stempel was practically allergic to confrontation and tended to avoid making difficult decisions, especially if they would place him in conflict with members of his inner circle.

I knew how much that must have frustrated Smale, a naturally decisive person who had learned early in his career not just how to make tough choices, but also the necessity of making them quickly, rather than allowing problems to fester.

Smale had, from the start, been careful to be as fair to Stempel as he possibly could and to avoid any perception that he was acting behind the CEO's back. When he reluctantly accepted the independent directors' "fact-finding mission," he had insisted that a clause be added to the end of the resolution the group voted on. It stipulated that, in addition to delivering his findings to the independent directors, he would also deliver the report to the chairman, Stempel.

Now, with the most consequential meeting of Stempel's career looming just days away, Smale invited the GM CEO to come see him at the P&G offices in Cincinnati, where he once again went through his report.

When he'd finished, and with the full extent of GM's troubles laid out before them, he told the confrontation-averse Stempel that confrontation was exactly what he should expect from the outside directors.

The meeting was going to be very tough, Smale said. The board didn't want a bunch of spreadsheets and charts. It had all the data it needed. What the directors wanted from Stempel was assurance that he, personally, was up to the challenge he was facing.

A few days later, Stempel came before the board, and Smale read out a statement that the outside directors had agreed on. A key section addressed what they wanted from the CEO:

> At this stage, we believe the CEO of GM must be a change maker. Someone who can face the organization, see its shortcomings, and lead the implementation of the massive changes which are essential to equip the Corporation to survive and prosper in a competitive world it never had previously encountered.

Our question to you, today, is whether you can, or want to, be such a leader. Some believe that the history and culture of GM in which you developed and advanced may be your worst enemy. That culture may well impede you from making those massive changes; from displacing people, organizations and systems which have worked in the past, but are now, we believe, impediments. You must ask yourself whether you are prepared to dismantle the bureaucracy we see as encasing GM and inhibiting its competitive strengths.

We certainly recognize your talents in knowing cars about as well as anyone; as well as your inherent integrity and honesty.

But, those qualities alone are not enough.

We realize, too, that you may disagree with our conclusions that GM today absolutely requires a change maker.

But, can you do what the Board considers to be necessary?

Stempel proceeded to do precisely what Smale had cautioned him not to. He had brought reams of paper with him and offered to go into deep detail about specific actions he had already taken. At one point, he had to be asked to stop reading aloud to the board from a lengthy report on the company's North American Automobile business.

When asked, Stempel confirmed he had not come to the meeting with new ideas. He was convinced that GM was already on the right track and that the board simply needed to be patient.

Asked about the executives that the outside directors wanted to terminate, Stempel expressed his confidence in all of them and said that he intended to keep them all on the job to help execute his turnaround plan — the same plan in which GM's senior managers, according to Smale's review, had no confidence.

Eventually, Stempel was asked to leave the meeting so that the directors could deliberate among themselves.

When the door shut behind the CEO, the outside directors looked at each other with varying levels of alarm. Stempel had, if possible, made matters worse.

After a lengthy discussion of the presentation, which the directors unanimously agreed had been gravely deficient, they began to consider next steps.

Smale was asked if he would be willing to continue his research into the state of the company and if he would accept election as chairman of the board's executive committee. The idea was to give him the authority to speak for the outside directors in his communication with GM management.

Seeing no alternative, Smale agreed.

Next, the board agreed that they would still demand the firing of several of the company's senior leaders. The directors also decided to elevate one of the company's rising stars, Jack Smith, who was currently running the company's international division, to a more senior role.

Smith, who had taken over an ailing GM Europe division years before and turned it around, would be named president and chief operating officer, giving him de facto oversight of the entirety of General Motors' car business.

It would be a harsh rebuke for Stempel, who would retain the titles of CEO and chairman of the board but lose day-to-day control over the heart of the business. The independent directors wanted to make it plain to him that he was on probation. Jack Smith was being brought in to make the kind of changes Stempel apparently could not. If he was unable to work with Smith, Stempel's future with GM was in question.

When the board finished deliberating, they summoned Stempel back to the meeting, where Millstein read out the resolution that had been agreed on.

Told that the board expected him to act promptly, Stempel signaled that he understood, and headed home to Detroit.

———

The morning after the meeting, Smale got a message from Stempel, saying that he wanted to take some time to consider how to make the changes the board had requested. He asked to speak with them at a previously scheduled meeting in Dallas the following weekend.

Smale agreed, but he was surprised several days later when his phone rang in Cincinnati and Stempel's secretary put her boss on the line.

Smale's eyes widened as the CEO outlined a plan that he had hatched with the members of his management committee to keep his top lieutenants on in new roles at GM.

Smale was stunned. The board wanted GM's management out because they had repeatedly proved themselves unable to turn around the domestic automobile business. The signal sent by handing them comfortable sinecures in Detroit after years of failure was exactly the opposite of what the board wanted to convey.

Stempel plainly wasn't getting the message.

———————

In Dallas the next week, Stempel met with the board and again asked that his team be allowed to remain at GM, but to be reassigned to other duties.

A frustrated group of directors dismissed Stempel and, for the second time in just over a week, began debating the future of the company's top management.

Stempel was clearly determined that no member of his management team would have to leave the company, even if they might be forced to swallow the very public humiliation of a demotion.

In a meeting that dragged on late into the night, the independent directors gave Stempel some of what he wanted, by allowing the CEO's team to stay on in reduced roles. However, they designated a new CFO, removed several members of Stempel's management team from the full board of directors and reasserted the new roles of both Jack Smith and Smale.

When the announcement was released to the press the following day, speculation immediately focused on Smale's new role as chairman of the executive committee of the board of directors. While Stempel remained the nominal chairman of GM, Smale's new job gave him effective control of the board's operations, leading to questions about who was actually running the company.

In response, Smale released a brief statement that read, "Contrary to recent media reports, neither I nor any of the other outside members of the General Motors Board of Directors intend to involve ourselves in the day-to-day business of GM. That job is the responsibility of Bob Stempel, and he has the board's full support and confidence in pursuing the goal to accelerate the return to profitability of GM's North American operations."

In researching this book, I read countless speeches by John Smale, articles in which he was quoted, and op-eds he had written. To the best of my knowledge, that statement of confidence in Stempel was as close as he ever came to telling a public lie.

I never resolved, in my own mind, Smale's treatment of Roger Smith and Bob Stempel during GM's years of crisis.

Once it became clear that Smith had lost the confidence of his board of directors, Smale and the outside GM board members continued to follow the CEO's lead on important issues — most notably, his selection of Stempel as his successor. Then, in the face of Stempel's multiple refusals to do what the board thought was necessary to save the company, Smale and his fellow board members left him in place — and declared public confidence in him — long past the point at which it would have made sense to replace him.

My only conclusion, and it's not one I find particularly satisfying, is that Smale felt that the CEO of a company deserved a greater degree of deference than other people when it came to decisions about its future. This would make some sense if Smale assumed that all CEOs felt the same weight of responsibility that he had when taking over P&G, and that they therefore could claim to have deeper insight into its operations and future.

Regardless of his reasons, though, Smale's days of deferring to Stempel were coming to an end.

Over the next several months, to the board's relief, Jack Smith began to do for North American operations what he had done in Europe. Within days of taking the job, Smith had assembled a strategy board, made up of the heads of various divisions. Working 12-hour days, the board began developing plans to cut costs by consolidating some of its diverse car engineering operations, reducing head-quarters staff and eliminating waste. Smith also upended the company's age-old purchasing policies, requiring that purchasing managers demand better pricing from suppliers and sever contracts with non-competitive producers.

Smale was delighted with Smith's progress. But he was significantly less happy with Bob Stempel. The CEO had, for months, continued to slow-walk the organizational changes at the very top of GM that the board had demanded. Letters from Smale to Stempel went unacknowledged, and requests for specific reports to the board were ignored.

In late June, speaking to the independent directors, Smale concluded that, rather than being moved to action by the events of the past seven months, Stempel was sulking.

"Unfortunately," Smale concluded, "Bob Stempel doesn't show any signs of being a change-maker."

Despite Smith's efforts, as the summer wore on, GM's financial situation continued to get worse. Both Smith and Smale were learning more about the inner workings of the company than they had known previously, and what they saw alarmed them.

Saturn, the new GM make introduced in 1990, was losing money rapidly, despite its initial success with consumers. At the same time, new accounting rules were about to force the company to take a massive charge of up to $20 billion against earnings in the coming year, to make up for a failure to set aside funds for retirees' health benefits.

What was thought to be a $300 million loss within GM's National Car Rental affiliate turned out to be a $1 billion write-off, on the heels of another $749 million write-off in the Hughes Aircraft division.

Then, in late August, GM's rocky relationship with the United Auto Workers union fell apart. Strategic strikes at part-making plants crippled production.

When the board met on Oct. 4, credit rating agencies were again threatening to downgrade GM's corporate debt, an action that could send the company into a death spiral.

Smale delivered a frank assessment of the company's position. "Our financial situation may be considerably worse than we thought it was going into last spring, or than it has so far been forecasted to be by the company," he said.

His presentation was a parade of horribles, not all of which were yet public knowledge. GM had been able to raise new capital through a stock offering earlier in the year, but it had already burned through most of it. Earnings forecasts were low and getting lower, and the company's debt-to-equity ratio was nearing 50%.

The new rules related to retiree health benefits could make it impossible for GM to issue stock dividends in the coming year, and Smith had determined that it would be necessary to close even more manufacturing facilities.

Reflecting the fact that so much information had been kept from the board in the past, Smale added, "I'm not sure what all this means, because I don't know how bad a situation we're actually in, or could be in shortly. And we're not helped by the proclivity of the company to hold discussions of their concerns and worries until the last minute and then surface with them, as has happened in the past."

Stempel, to this point, had not been in the meeting. Smale, however, had deputized Harry Pearce to give the CEO a detailed breakdown of the issues that Smale had placed before the outside directors.

After Stempel arrived, Smale reiterated the number of pressing issues facing the company and demanded to know what Stempel planned to do about it.

Stempel merely repeated what had, at this point, become his default response to everything. The board simply needed to have patience. Plans were already in place to turn GM around. There was no need to panic.

If Stempel believed what he was saying, he was the only one in the room who did.

The increasingly precarious position of General Motors was becoming clear to the financial press, and rumors began to circulate that the board of directors was about to push out Stempel.

One after another, reporters at major newspapers filed stories predicting Stempel's imminent departure. One by one, they were rebutted by GM's public relations office, which pointed out that, in every case, the stories were based on anonymous sources. But the drumbeat continued, and the one voice that could have silenced the speculation — John Smale's — was silent.

———

Peter Smale was visiting his parents in Cincinnati one evening in late October when the phone rang. It was late for someone to be calling, but that wasn't unusual in the Smale household at the time. The turmoil at GM had long since spilled out of Smale's office and into his home. News reports were rife with speculation that Bob Stempel was about to be ousted.

Peter saw his father step into his office to take the call, then step out again, quiet and grim.

He sensed that something important had happened, but he also knew that his father was extremely close-mouthed when it came to the internal discussions of the GM board. Weeks later, after the subject of the call was no longer material information, Peter reminded his father of it.

"Who was it?" Peter asked.

It had been Bob Stempel, Smale replied.

Peter pressed. "What did he want?"

"He wanted me to call the press and reassure them that the board of directors has confidence in him."

Peter waited, expectantly.

"I couldn't," Smale said. "I said, 'I can't do that, Bob.'"

"What did he say?" Peter asked.

"He was quiet for a moment, and then he said, 'Okay. Okay John, I understand.'"

On the morning of Oct. 22, John Smale finally broke his silence on the question of Stempel's fate, issuing a terse statement that read, "The GM Board of Directors has taken no action regarding any management changes at GM. However, the question of executive leadership is a primary concern to the Board of Directors of any company, and GM is no exception. The GM Board of Directors continues to carefully reflect upon the wisest course for assuring the most effective leadership for the corporation."

Bob Stempel had missed many signs and signals at the helm of General Motors, but he couldn't ignore this one. It was a very clear, very public, no-confidence vote from the board of directors, delivered by the man the directors had designated as their leader.

At his office in Detroit, Bob Stempel sat down and began drafting his resignation letter.

That resignation, on a Monday in late October 1992, set off an avalanche of speculation about the future of General Motors. The basic shape of the new management team wasn't really in question. It was widely assumed, correctly, that Smale would be elected chairman of the board and that Jack Smith, until now the CEO in all but title, would formally take the reins of the business.

In the days between Smale's statement to the press and Stempel's resignation, Jack Smith got a call from Smale's secretary asking for a meeting. The two men drove to a hotel halfway between Detroit and Cincinnati.

When I spoke with Smith, he said that, up to that point, he had known Smale only casually. Smith was on GM's board, but as the head of the company's international operations, he had frequently been away from Detroit.

In that meeting, Smith told me, he was immediately struck by the force of Smale's personality. "I had never run into anybody quite like him," he recalled.

At that point, Smale had accumulated more knowledge about the working of General Motors than many of the company's senior executives. He impressed Smith with his deep understanding of the business and his willingness to ask difficult questions about its future.

Smale told Smith that the board wanted him to take over as CEO. But before Smith accepted, he told Smale he had an important issue that the two of them needed to address.

Smale was in the process of ousting one GM CEO and taking over the entire board of directors. Smith needed to know what he was being asked to do. Would he be a real CEO, with all the authority that came with the job? Or would he be expected to defer to Smale on decisions related to the business?

Smith said that Smale made it abundantly clear. "He did not want to run the company," Smith told me.

Smith continued, "You know, these things don't always work very well, but in this case it was fantastic because he was disciplined, he asked tough questions, but he did his homework and he wasn't seeking the limelight or anything like that. He was just a really honest, tough guy."

———————

Smale viewed the coming weeks as especially sensitive and understood that Smith's concern about appearances was valid. As the leader of a boardroom revolt, once Smale became chairman, there would be an assumption among many — not least of all in the ranks of GM's employees — that he was the real boss.

"One of the first things that needed to be clear, importantly for the organization, but also for the world at large, was who was going to be running General Motors," Smale later said.

The board of directors formalized Smale's and Smith's new titles in a regularly scheduled meeting the following Monday. The board also accepted the resignations of most of the company's top leadership, clearing the way for Smith to name his own team.

After the board meeting, Smale and Smith immediately sat down to deliver a live video address to GM's employees across the country.

With the other members of the board of directors seated behind them, the two men sat side by side and addressed the company's workers. As they planned in advance, Smale said far less than Smith, and he nodded when the new CEO made it unequivocally clear who would be running the company on a day-to-day basis.

"He will not run the company," Smith said, with a look toward Smale. "I will."

To emphasize the point, when a post-meeting press conference was convened, Smale did not appear at all, leaving Smith to become the public face of the new GM management team. Other board members were deputized to stress with reporters that Smith, and not the board of directors, would be running the company.

Smale, one of the other board members pointed out, would not even have an office in Detroit but would work from P&G headquarters in Cincinnati.

The General Motors board's ouster of Bob Stempel was an inflection point in the history of corporate governance.

The events at GM in the fall of 1992 were soon mirrored by other companies. Board members at American Express, Eastman Kodak, Westinghouse and IBM all rose up soon afterward and fired their companies' leadership. The rebellions didn't stop there, either, extending to smaller companies including Quaker State, CompUSA, and many more.

At the same time that Smith was working to make GM competitive again, Smale and his fellow board members were formalizing the changes that the board had made to the way it operated over the previous year.

In the years prior to the boardroom revolt at GM, the typical corporate board was a largely deferential group of business leaders, selected because they lent prestige to the company by their presence, though their legal responsibility was to represent the interests of the shareholders.

Smale's own thinking about the responsibilities of the board of directors had been evolving for several years prior to the revolt at GM.

In a letter to Ira Millstein the previous June, Smale wrote, "I've always felt it would be possible to operate with a chairman being a non-employee director; but, that would complicate the CEO's job. I'm coming, however, more and more to the point of view that this is a configuration that could lead to more effective corporate governance — at least in those situations in which the corporation is in trouble."

In the event that a company wants to retain a direct employee of the firm as the chairman of the board, he said, there needed to be a way for the outside directors to "bring focus" to their activities. "In the absence of an appointed 'leader,' there is no easy way to bring initiative to the considerations of the outside directors."

The concept of a "lead director" was one that, over the coming decades, would be widely adopted across public companies in the United States.

In 1993, Smale and the other outside directors at GM began hammering out a new set of guidelines for how the board would conduct business. The months-long process resulted in a set of 28 rules, covering everything from how many members the board ought to have to the committee structure to the frequency and length of meetings.

More importantly, though, the rules specified that the CEO of General Motors served at the pleasure of the board of directors and that the board should be free to determine who held the position of CEO and the position of board chair "any way that seems best for the Company at a given point in time."

The guidelines called for regularly scheduled meetings of the outside directors and annual reviews of the performance of all senior executives. It codified that board documents were to be distributed prior to meetings and that individual board members have "complete access" to senior management.

While Smale and his fellow board members largely saw the guidelines as a formalization of their new procedures, the larger business world saw them as a foundational document for a new age of corporate governance.

"A Magna Carta for Directors," the magazine *Businessweek* boomed in a headline. Within months, the California Public Employees' Retirement System, among the largest investors in the country, had sent a letter to the 200 largest U.S. companies, asking them to provide the internal guidelines for their own boards of directors or, at least, to say whether their boards met the same standards as the General Motors board. Six months later, CalPERS revealed the results, grading the cream of corporate America, on a scale of A-plus to F, on their corporate governance practices.

In October 1994, in recognition of how the changes at GM had spread out across corporate America, the National Association of Corporate Directors named Smale its "Director of the Year," at a dinner in Washington, D.C.

In a speech that evening, Smale spelled out the fundamental role of the members of a corporate board in a way that drew a direct contrast with the behavior of the GM board during the Roger Smith years.

> The basic responsibility of the board is to represent the owners' interest in successfully perpetuating the business. The board is responsible for seeing that the corporation is managed in such a way as to ensure this result. I see this as an active, not a passive, responsibility.
>
> It is incumbent on the board to ensure, in good times as well as difficult ones, that the management is capably executing its responsibilities. The board encourages competent management by the nature of its questions and its requests for information. Also, by the depth of its understanding of the company's vision and how the company executes its strategies.
>
> As I see it, the board has to act as an independent auditor of management ... asking the tough questions that management might not

ask itself, particularly when the company is doing well and seen to be an industry leader.

In the speech, Smale pointedly took issue with news reports that had described the changes at General Motors as having been a "power grab" by the board of directors and suggesting that management now had less control over day-to-day operation of the business than it had before.

"Strong boards can be a source of strength to management ... a source of competitive advantage to the company," Smale said, adding that "my greatest reward on the GM board will be the success of Jack Smith and his team."

————————

Smith's successes at GM came quickly. Cost-cutting and plant closures earned much of the attention at first, but by 1994, GM had an excellent story to tell.

The business was generating $12 billion more in annual cash flow than it had just three years previously and had exceeded expectations by generating a profit — before interest, taxes, and retiree health-care costs — of $511 million, compared to a loss of $170 million a year previously.

Market share was on the rise. The company had redesigned cars across almost all of its different nameplates, and Chevrolet would announce a new design every six months for the next six years.

The company's Hughes Electronics division was about to test-launch a satellite television service that would eventually morph into the successful DirecTV service.

GM was also able to claim a rare victory over its domestic rivals in the push to open Asian markets, particularly China. As part-owner of a $100 million joint venture in China, the company was far ahead of the competition there, and it announced that it was in final talks to open Chinese plants that would make minivans and subcompacts. Additionally, the company said that, by year's end, it would open factories to produce cars in India and Indonesia.

These early successes marked the beginning of what would become one of the most remarkable business turnarounds in U.S. history. The company had turned the corner on profitability and was beginning to claw back some of the market share lost over the previous decade.

Jack Smith had pulled a promising young executive named Rick Wagoner from his job running operations in Brazil and made him the new CFO of the company. I was anxious to speak with Wagoner because I knew that, given GM's perilous financial state, he would have spent considerable time with Smale.

At 39, Wagoner was the most junior of the new management team. And though he would eventually become CEO of GM himself, at the time he was more focused on absorbing as much knowledge from Smale and Smith as he could.

Wagoner told me that one of the things that struck him about Smale's approach to turning around the struggling automaker was the broadness of his vision.

"It was clear to me that he viewed his role as bigger than coming in as a board member and making sure the company improved its financial results," Wagoner told me. "He was always talking about bigger stuff: about building brands, employee engagement, product enhancements for the benefit of customers."

Smale, Wagoner said, constantly reminded GM's senior management that the main objective was to ensure that General Motors continued to exist as a successful and growing company far into the future.

He would arrive in Detroit with a folder full of news clippings and other documents and would pepper Smith, Wagoner, and other members of the GM executive committee with questions about their strategy for the future and their reasoning behind specific decisions.

"He would lead with questions," Wagoner told me. "He would ask good questions, he would ask tough questions. He wasn't afraid to challenge, but once you satisfied him, he was just a terrific supporter."

As with many people who knew Smale well, Wagoner wanted to be sure I understood that, beneath a stoic exterior, was a friendly and often funny person.

In his early days as CFO, Wagoner told me, he occupied a strangely configured office tucked in a corner of GM's executive suite. One of the perks of the office was that it had its own private bathroom.

One day, after Smale and Wagoner had finished a meeting, Smale excused himself and stepped into Wagoner's bathroom. The CFO thought nothing of it until later in the day, when he entered the bathroom himself. On the countertop near the sink were a few odds and ends, but something new caught Wagoner's eye.

Looking down he saw a note, in Smale's handwriting, protruding from underneath Wagoner's tube of Colgate toothpaste, the rival of Procter & Gamble's Crest.

"Be careful," Smale had written. "This stuff will kill you."

———

Above all, Wagoner told me that the most remarkable thing he witnessed during those years was Smale's relationship with Jack Smith.

At the time, the two men were testing an uncommon arrangement of having a non-executive chairman of the board of directors, at a time when the chairman and CEO roles were typically vested in the same person.

"The problem with that system is you can get clashes of egos," Wagoner said. "But this was exactly the opposite. These are both two guys who are capable, successful, but not long on personal ego. And so they, I thought, set a great example of working together and respecting each other's boundaries, and each other's input, but effectively doing their jobs."

Years later, Wagoner would sit down and write a letter to Smale, on his embossed GM stationery identifying him as president and CEO of the company. I found it in Smale's files several weeks after I spoke with Wagoner.

Reflecting on the turnaround, he wrote, "I feel like I had a 'front row seat' in observing the best businessman I've ever encountered teach us all how to revive a business — one that you had personally not grown up in — and completely change it into a modern business model ready to attack future opportunities."

———

Near the end of my conversation with Wagoner, he reminded me of a speech that Smale gave in 1995, after he announced that he would step back from the role of chairman of General Motors and hand it off to Jack Smith. As dictated by the board guidelines drafted a few years before, Smale would become the chairman of the executive committee of the board, or the "lead" director.

While the change didn't reflect the end of his relationship with the company — Smale would remain on the GM board for five more years — there was a valedictory quality to the speech he delivered to the company's North American Operations leadership meeting in November of that year.

Smale spoke about his long career in business and how he had discovered that many of the things he treasured about Procter & Gamble were present in General Motors:

> Procter & Gamble always seemed to me — almost like a living thing. Certainly, it had character — a meaning. And somehow, although the essence of a company's personality and character is the sum of those of the people who have been part of it, I've always viewed P&G as more than the sum of its individuals.
>
> Now I think about GM the same way. We as individuals have faults, and we make mistakes. But the company doesn't — or, at least, shouldn't. Its principles should reflect the best of us as individuals, without the faults. It should reflect the unrelenting drive for and the insistence upon excellence — on winning; the excitement of innovation — or risk-taking — of bringing new ideas and product innovation to the world's consumers.
>
> Would Procter & Gamble have been different if I hadn't been there? Maybe, maybe not. I don't know. Would the world have been different without Procter & Gamble and its innovative products? I truly believe it would. And, if I had some hand in that, then the company has given a meaning to my life's work that will outlive me.

Near the end of his remarks, Smale presented a manifesto of sorts, possibly the fullest articulation he ever delivered about what he believed a company — one with a soul — ought to look like.

> I'm proud to be connected with a company that wants to be the best; that wants to be a leader in everything it does; and is willing to embrace the high standards necessary to consistently achieve high goals.

> I want to work with a company that places integrity above all else. A company that believes in always trying to do the right thing; always obeys the law — even when our competitors might not. A company that always practices fair dealings with its customers, its dealers, its suppliers.

> I want to work with a company that operates by principle — and is willing to forgo expedient compromise to preserve its principles. A company that stands up for these principles. A company that would rather forgo a sale or a deal than make a payment under the table or discriminate between our customers.

> I want to work with a company that places the quality of its products and the safety of those products, as well as the safety of its workforce, above all other considerations.

> I want to work with a company that is unequivocally proactive, not just responsive in its efforts to clean up and preserve the world's environment.

> And, I want to work with a company that puts character above all the other qualities in the people that it hires. I want to work with a company that honors and respects individual initiatives at every level of the business.

And, I want to work for a company that is dedicated to the development of its people. A company that believes in the fair treatment of its employees.

Then, addressing the audience directly, Smale continued.

"I don't, of course, know it for a fact, but I suspect perhaps 50 years or more ago, some of these same principles, using different words, may have been articulated at a meeting like this of GM managers. All of the GM people who would have heard those comments are, of course, gone from the company. And, 50 years from now, at a meeting like this one, GM people will gather to discuss the same values — but all of us will be gone from the company.

"GM's people will come and go, but the values that bind this organization — this institution — must be permanent. They can never change. And these kinds of values are more than ethical principles: They are good business. And they are rules of living that make one's career rewarding beyond material gain."

———

Reflecting on that speech, it occurred to me that Smale's time at General Motors, first preparing the ground for Jack Smith and his team to take over, and then working with the new executive team to save GM from crisis, was really a distillation of who Smale was as a person and as a businessman.

He had identified a company in trouble and took personal responsibility for finding and implementing a solution. That it meant long hours and taking on onerous responsibilities was no barrier. He threw himself into saving General Motors the way he would have if it had been his own beloved Procter & Gamble. He hadn't done it for the money — he had plenty of that. He hadn't done it for the spotlight — he actively avoided that.

He had done it because, in General Motors, Smale saw more than business units and profit-and-loss statements. As with P&G, he saw an entity that gave the people who worked for it a sense of belonging to something larger than themselves.

224

He saw a company that had a proud history of trying to make the world a better place. A company that transformed itself into a key component of the "arsenal of democracy" to help the Allies win World War II. A company that had created the first airbag, saving countless lives. A company that invented the catalytic converter, helping to reduce air pollution.

He also saw a company that had pulled generations of families into the middle class and kept them there. One with a network of retirees who depended on it to support them in their old age.

Smale saw GM as an institution that, like P&G, deserved to be perpetuated. He had worked to save it because he believed, simply, that it was the right thing to do.

CHAPTER 18

Moving Through Waters, Straight-Backed, Facing Forward

After retiring from P&G, Smale spent much of the 1990s occupied with the turnaround at General Motors. However, he remained a regular and steadying presence in the halls of Procter & Gamble, where he still came to the office most days when he was in Cincinnati.

It was not uncommon for company executives to find a note from Smale in their inboxes, praising a particular speech or deft business decision. Many told me that they held on to those hand-written missives for decades after.

Smale's door was always open to the P&G CEOs who followed him, and they frequently sought him out for counsel. But the interactions almost always went in one direction, with Smale's successors seeking his advice, rather than Smale actively offering it. Once he stepped away from the executive suite, Smale didn't try to force his way back inside.

John Pepper, who took over as CEO in 1995, often asked for Smale's opinion on business decisions, but he told me he could recall only one time when Smale reached out to him.

It was early in Pepper's time as CEO, and a difficult decision had resulted in a punishing hit to the company's share price, driving it down by more than 5%.

Pepper's secretary called in to his office and told him that Smale was on the line.

"John," Smale said. "I'm thinking you might be looking at the share price."

"Yeah, John, I did notice it," Pepper said grimly.

"Well, stop looking at it," Smale said. "You're doing the right things. You just keep going on the plan you have. It's the right plan. Just keep going, and don't worry about the stock price. It'll take care of itself."

———————

As Smale gradually stepped back from business and dedicated more and more time to his wife and family, there were regular reminders of the successes that had brought him to the pinnacle of the business world.

In 1996, he was inducted into the National Business Hall of Fame. In 2002, the American Advertising Federation Hall of Fame inducted him, as well. He received the Great Living Cincinnatian Award from the Cincinnati Chamber of Commerce in February 1997, and beyond that he had amassed a wall full of honorary doctorates from various universities.

To Smale, though, the prize that really mattered was the continued success of Procter & Gamble. In the years after he left the company, Ed Artzt, John Pepper and the CEOs who followed them began building on the foundation he had laid.

In Europe, the company pressed east, opening markets not just in the satellite states of the former Soviet Union but in Russia itself. By 1997, the company was generating $1.3 billion in revenue in Central and Eastern Europe — markets that had been nonexistent only a decade before — and was far outpacing competition that had been slow to see the potential for growth there.

In Central and South America, P&G had prospered. With operations from Guatemala in the north to Chile and Argentina in the south, P&G sales in Latin America more than quadrupled over the course of a decade, from $502 million in 1986 to $2.2 billion in 1996.

Early efforts to open the Chinese markets to P&G's products were beginning to see success, as were expansions throughout Southeast Asia and, increasingly, into Africa.

Fewer than 20 years after Smale asked Artzt to "take us global," P&G was truly a global company, with markets totaling some 5.25 billion consumers, or about 88% of the world's population.

By the turn of the century, P&G would have net sales of $40 billion, nearly four times the $10.7 billion the company had when Smale took over in the early '80s.

Fittingly, John Smale's final meeting as a member of the P&G board of directors was held outside the United States, in Mexico.

At the event, he delivered remarks that the executives he had led and mentored over the decades would remember for years afterward.

He began not by citing sales figures or profits but by honoring his wife, Phyllis.

"I am one of the world's most fortunate people," he said. "Arguably the two most important decisions we make in life involve the person with whom we share our life and the nature of our life's work. Fifty years ago this fall, I met and fell in love with a redhead. She was warm and open and outgoing. I can't imagine what my life would have been like without her. Certainly it would have been greatly diminished."

The second decision, of course, was where Smale chose to spend what he called "a working life." He reminded them of his career, and the twist of fate that had him searching for a new job just as an opening arose at P&G in 1952.

His immediate recognition of the character of the company and of the executives who led it became a touchstone for Smale and the foundation of his belief that Procter & Gamble was more than just a company. That it was — and needed to be cared for — like a living thing.

His final charge to the executives and board members was to remember that.

"I believe the fundamental responsibility of this Management — and of the board of Procter & Gamble — is the successful perpetuation of this institution.

Managers — and directors — will come and go. Shareholders will change. Certainly, the world in which we exist will change. We'll have good years of business growth, and some that won't be so good. The things that must not change are the basic principles of this company. Those precepts that are articulated in our Statement of Purpose.

"By following these principles, this company has grown and its employees and shareholders have profited ... and I'm confident this generation of management and directors will continue to follow these principles. And all the rest — as it has in the past — will follow."

—————

When I started writing this book, right through to the completion of the first draft, my intention had been to close it with the end of John Smale's business career. He had stepped away from the board of directors of Procter & Gamble in 1995, the same year he stepped down as chairman of GM, though he remained lead director there until 2000.

But after it became clear that a true examination of Smale's life would require going beyond his role as a business leader, I began to wonder what his life had looked like after the trappings of business leadership were stripped away. When there were no more corporate jets, no more board meetings, no more senior executives hanging on his every word, what would have been left of John Smale's life?

He had been 68 when he stepped away from the board of Procter & Gamble — by no means a young man but not ancient, either. He was not quite 73 when he ended his tenure at GM in 2000. Again, not young but still vigorous enough to have been on the same trip to the Cascapédia as my father three years later, in 2003.

What I found was that, as Smale and Phyllis remade their life together, away from the regular involvement with the ins and outs of corporate America, some things changed, but much did not.

For the Smales, what remained in this new life was their relationships with other people and, most importantly, their relationship with each other.

On a trip to Cincinnati, I finished up my interviews late one afternoon and decided to see for myself a spot in the city that Cathy had told me about, a place very special to the Smale family.

Among the Smales, it's known as the "anniversary garden," but if it has an official name, I couldn't find it. Cathy had pointed it out to me one day while we were driving out of downtown.

The park sits where Columbia Parkway and one of its off-ramps split apart, forming two sides of a vague triangle, bounded on the third by the on-ramp to Interstate 71. It's the sort of unusable space in a city that might normally fall into neglect and become the collection point for litter and debris from the thousands of cars that rush past it every day. But drivers, if they notice the space at all, instead see neatly manicured shrubs and plants and, next to a small pine tree, a sculpture of two geese, flying side by side.

My problem was that I didn't know how to get to it. In my rental car I could get close, zooming past it on the way out of town, or coming back, but there was no convenient place to stop.

Finally, I worked my way under the web of ramps and bypasses, and found myself on Butler Street, next to a heavily fenced-in parking lot, and spotted the sloping path beneath Columbia Parkway that leads to the park.

The reason this miniature park exists at all is that John and Phyllis Smale adopted it, setting aside enough money to pay for continued maintenance by the city. A small plaque, attached to a stone, sits unobtrusively along the path up to the park, describing the donation as a gift to the city of Cincinnati on the occasion of the couple's 50th wedding anniversary.

Climbing further, I came out level with the parkway and found the statue: four feet tall, cast in bronze and set on a granite base of nearly the same height. Close up, it's clear that the birds are not just geese but Canada geese, a nod to Smale's country of birth. The two figures, soaring side by side with wings overlapping, appear to skim above a curling wave.

A different plaque on the base indicates that the sculpture was commissioned by the Smales' children, as a 50th-anniversary gift. The significance of the two geese would be invisible to the casual passerby. However, Cathy had told me the story behind it.

Decades before, at Christmastime, Smale had gone to a jeweler and asked for a custom order. He wanted a one-of-a-kind gold pendant made for his wife. At Smale's specific instruction, the jeweler created a silhouette of two geese, side by side, with their necks entwined.

On Christmas, Phyllis opened a box to find the pendant alongside a brief, handwritten note from her husband, explaining the gift's significance. It read, "Geese mate for life."

Though few who encountered him in his public role would have known it, John Smale was a deeply sentimental man, even to the point of provoking the occasional eye roll from his wife, as she suffered through his playing Gershwin's "My One and Only" over and over again.

Their mutual devotion to one another was obvious to everyone who met them. Even during his working years, it had not been unusual for P&G employees to encounter their CEO walking hand in hand with Phyllis near their home, often stopping for ice cream at Graeter's, a Cincinnati institution only a few decades younger than Procter & Gamble.

At the same time, Smale was keenly aware of the price that Phyllis had paid for the life they enjoyed.

In a letter to Cathy many years later, Smale recalled that Phyllis had never been comfortable with the role his job placed her in outside the home.

"Phyllis was very much her own person in a situation where that became incredibly difficult," he wrote. "She never became a 'corporate wife,' although she was in many ways the ideal one. She charmed people with cheerfulness and openness." This, he added, even though, "she didn't like the role of the CEO's wife."

But beyond making command appearances at dinners and business trips, Smale recognized that Phyllis had created a home life that made it possible for him to run a global organization.

"She allowed me to focus on what I was doing for a living," he said in an interview. "I guess there are some people who can focus on more than one thing at once. I mean, they can have a difficult home life and still do well in the business world. I couldn't do that. I was just not built that way. She raised our four kids. She was her own person. She was bright, attractive, but independent-minded."

He added, "I was so comfortable in my relationship with Phyllis and so at ease that there was no tension. The home life was totally supportive. I don't know what life would have been like, had I not had her."

———

As the Smales' 50th anniversary approached, their children commissioned Cincinnati artist John Leon to create the sculpture — called "Synchronicity" — in honor of their parents.

Leon explained the symbolism of his work this way: "The Canada geese symbolize being mated for life, taking long journeys together, and of course, Canada, [John Smale's] homeland. The birds' overlapping wings become one in the composition to convey their unity. The base forms an upward spiral, a symbol of eternity. The etched lines from the base carry over onto the wings, their crisscrossing further uniting the individual birds."

The Smales were charmed by the work and had two additional copies of it cast. But the best place for the original, they decided, was in the little spot along the highway that they had taken to calling their "anniversary garden."

The miniature park is not the Smales' biggest contribution to the city of Cincinnati. That would be Smale Riverfront Park. In some ways, though, that tiny speck of a garden near the highway is the perfect testament to John and Phyllis Smale's commitment to the city.

Like the water lines, streets, and electrical grid that are still maintained under the rules established by the Smale Commission, and the multiple urban green spaces created by Phyllis and backed by her own fundraising efforts, the little park doesn't carry their name. It just offers a small bit of beauty, accessible to all Cincinnatians. The anniversary garden is a quiet reminder of the countless ways, big and small, that the Smales left their mark on Cincinnati.

———————

By the time Smale retired, the family had established two different retreats outside of Cincinnati that would become the focus of much of their social and family life.

While he was still running P&G, Smale had taken up a colleague on an offer to visit his family's house on McGregor Bay, in the northern part of Lake Huron in Ontario. Smale had been so taken with the natural beauty of the area — and with the excellent fishing — that, within a few years, he purchased an island in the bay and began construction of a large home. The Smales' property on the bay eventually extended to three houses on a trio of nearby islands.

Even in retirement, Smale was not able to abandon some of the habits that he had developed over his working life, and that included a strict schedule. When grandchildren overslept, Smale woke them at what he deemed the appropriate hour by singing, "When the Red, Red Robin Comes Bob-Bob-Bobbin' Along." At McGregor Bay, the dinner schedule was set in stone, and woe to any family member who forgot it. Dinner was served promptly at 7, and nobody left the table until the last person was finished eating. Whichever family members had cooked the evening's meal were free from cleanup duties.

Smale also encouraged everyone to spend time each day working on the property, whether that meant maintaining the boats, tending the garden or cleaning the boathouse.

There was also, occasionally, some P&G "brand promotion" work to do. One summer when two of the grandchildren, Sam and Emma Durham, spent several weeks at the house with the Smales, they teased John about a neon pink windbreaker that he kept there.

The jacket was a promotional giveaway that P&G had produced in the color of one of its best-known brands, Pepto-Bismol. When the family went to the nearby town for supplies, Smale offered Sam 25 cents to wear the jacket in order to "raise brand awareness." Sam earned several dollars during their stay, but to Smale, the amusement was priceless.

Reading through letters and other documents, I came to understand that, to John and Phyllis, McGregor Bay was more than just a vacation home. As with so much of what Smale had done in his business career, he and Phyllis had built their second home in Canada with an eye on the future — specifically, the future of their family. The house was meant to be a sort of magnet that would draw their children and grandchildren back, keeping the Smale family together after John and Phyllis were gone.

Late in life, he told his extended family that, after he died, the best way they could honor his and Phyllis's memory was to "stay committed as a family."

Going a step further, he also arranged that no future inheritor of the property could profit by selling it. The proceeds from any sale would go to the Smale Family Foundation.

In addition to the home in Canada, the Smales established a home in Marathon, Fla. where they could spend part of each winter.

Both homes, in the years after Smale's retirement, would become waypoints for dozens of friends and former co-workers, whose relationship with the Smales transcended their years at P&G or General Motors.

The compound in Florida, in particular, was a regular stopping place for former P&G colleagues of Smale's, many of whom had purchased their own retirement properties in South Florida.

In interview after interview, former P&G and General Motors executives told me about how the Smales welcomed them into their homes. As time passed, the layers of hierarchy and deference built up during the years of working for Smale gradually wore thin, then disappeared altogether.

Former colleagues who had been too far down in the ranks of leadership during Smale's career to glimpse the man behind the title of CEO or chairman began to see the John Smale that only the inner circle of management had known during his working career. His sense of humor was given free rein, he seemed to relish interacting with people who weren't afraid to disagree with him, and old relationships, instead of attenuating with age and distance, instead grew deeper and more meaningful.

Cathy told me that something similar happened with Smale's relationship with his grandchildren.

"My father softened and relaxed with his grandchildren eventually," she said. That was especially obvious in his relationship with Cathy's youngest daughter, Madeline, who is several years younger than the other grandchildren.

"She was raised around a less stern grandfather," Cathy said. "She teased him, and he teased her. She totally charmed him, and he responded to her natural playfulness."

———————

Sadly, the Smales' life together in retirement did not last nearly as long as either had hoped. A year after Smale left the board of General Motors, Phyllis was diagnosed with cancer.

When it became clear that no treatment offered her a chance of survival, Phyllis began one final project: preparing her husband for life without her.

She insisted that he learn to cook seven different meals, one for each night of the week, and began teaching him the basics of managing a house. It was eye-opening for Smale, his friends told me. He had spent so many decades being "managed," both in the office and at home, that there were major gaps in his knowledge of day-to-day life that needed to be filled.

Phyllis didn't limit her work on Smale to remedial home economics. She pressed their friends, Rich and Marje Kiley, to make sure that, after she died, Smale would continue to see people, travel and maintain a healthy social life.

No preparation, though, was enough to cushion the blow when Phyllis passed away just after Christmas in 2006. Smale was utterly devastated. Across hundreds of hours of interviews with his friends and family, I never heard anyone describe a moment when Smale was overcome by emotion, with the exception of that day.

When I asked Ed Artzt about it, his face darkened, and all he said was, "That was a terrible day."

In the years that followed Phyllis's death, Smale, much as his wife had wished, continued to live his life. He maintained his relationships with friends and colleagues, often with the help of the Kileys, who arranged dinners and trips, and made sure that Smale, now entering his early 80s, remained active.

Smale also retained his sense of humor. Marje Kiley told me that in the years after Phyllis's death, when he began cooking meals for himself, he developed the habit of leaving the kitchen cabinets wide open. This frustrated Marje, herself a gourmet cook who keeps an immaculate kitchen, and she constantly gave Smale grief about it.

As payback, Smale went to the Kileys' home while they were away, let himself in, and methodically opened every single cabinet in the entire house.

But to those who knew him best, it was plain that he missed Phyllis, terribly, every day. When a hurricane destroyed a garden installation she had overseen outside their Florida home, he spent years working to bring it back to match her vision.

With time, the signs of the disease that would eventually take his life became impossible to ignore.

Pulmonary fibrosis turns the lungs into scar tissue. First, it robs its victims of the ability to exert themselves; later, it makes even the most mundane activities feel like exertion.

I knew from my discussions with Cathy and other members of the family that Smale's experience of the disease had been quite different from my father's. For Smale, the progress of the disease was slower, if no less relentless.

When his doctor prescribed physical therapy, meant to increase his ability to take advantage of the lung function he had left, Smale threw himself into it with the same sort of determination he would have focused on an underperforming P&G brand.

When it became necessary for him to be on oxygen, the metal canister with the cannula leading to his nose simply became part of Smale's routine. He didn't complain and didn't limit his activities — he simply adapted.

In November 2010, P&G CEO Bob McDonald announced that the company would dedicate the auditorium in the company's headquarters building to Smale. It was a major statement of how vital Smale's legacy was, more than 20 years after he had stepped down as CEO.

By that time, Smale had lost so much weight that he had to arrange a special trip to Brooks Brothers to have a new suit fitted. But on the appointed day, he arrived at P&G headquarters, accompanied by many family members, for the dedication.

I've spoken to at least a dozen people who were there for the dedication of the auditorium. What they remember about that day is not the remarks delivered by P&G executives or the glowing tribute video that the company produced in Smale's honor.

What they remember is that, when the ceremony was over and Smale saw the line of people forming to speak with him, the former CEO got to his feet, oxygen tank in tow, and stood there for as long as it took to shake every hand, listen to every story and return every greeting.

These were Smale's people, and he loved them the way he loved P&G. In his view, they were entitled to his respect and his courtesy. Doing anything other than standing to greet them would have been unthinkable.

That evening, at dinner with his family, Cathy remembered how her father's mood seemed to have lightened and how exhilarated he had been to spend time with current P&G employees.

Thinking about Smale and how his relationships with friends and family deepened in his later years, I came back again to Chris Caldemeyer, Smale's grandson. Over more than two years of researching, writing and rewriting, I became increasingly convinced that the relationship between John and Chris, in many ways, completed Smale as a character in his own story.

Unlike so many of the people in his life, Smale had, in his grandson, a relationship uncomplicated by the many factors that had necessarily influenced his connections with others.

Separated from his grandson by an entire generation, his relationship with Chris was stripped of the parent-child dynamic that complicated his relationship with Cathy and her siblings. As Smale set down the responsibilities of running P&G and General Motors, he was more available to his grandson than he had been to his own children.

Importantly, there was also very little that Chris wanted from his own life that Smale was in a position to give. Chris, as he passed from high school and into college, understood that what he wanted was to be a writer and a teacher — two paths that Smale had little chance of smoothing for him with money or connections.

Their shared love of fishing gave them the reason, if reason was needed, to spend time together. And, as any fisherman will tell you, the nature of time spent together on the water, or reviewing the day's successes and failures, is qualitatively different from time spent in most other pursuits.

I already knew the truth of that from time spent with my father, and when I came across a letter that Chris had written to his grandfather, it only confirmed it for me.

"The first thing that I want to say is that I love you," it begins. "It's strange to think how unfamiliar it is for most people to say those words, as we generally take it as a given, something that is so intrinsic to our relationships that it doesn't necessarily need saying. Although I'm sure you know I love you, it can't hurt much to tell you."

I didn't have to check the date on the letter to know what I was reading. By early 2011, it had become clear that Smale was losing his battle against pulmonary fibrosis and didn't have much longer to live.

This was Chris, who knew that his grandfather was dying, making sure that nothing was left unsaid between them.

I thought back to a similar conversation that I had with my father, and the words could not have felt more familiar.

"I want you to know how important you've been in my education of becoming a man," Chris wrote. "I can honestly say (and I really do think about this more often than you'll ever imagine) that whenever I'm faced with a problem, I ask myself, 'What would Grandpa do in this circumstance?'"

He continued, "You've shown me how to be courageous, honest and kind. You've taught me the value of trusting myself and my own character, something I've found many people have a hard time doing. And what's always astonished me is how effortless you made it seem."

Not long after he wrote that letter, Chris told me, he visited his grandfather in Florida, and they went fishing. Smale, at that point, was too weak to fish for very long and spent much of the day watching his grandson cast for permit, a notoriously difficult fish to catch.

"I actually somehow managed to hook and catch a permit on the fly, and I swear, he was happier than I was," Chris remembered. "The joy on his face was ... it was like a kid. Literally, like a child."

When I think about the end of John Smale's life, I prefer not to dwell on his final days. I was not there, but I know from painful experience what it must have been like.

Instead, I think about an evening that Chris Caldemeyer told me about, months before his grandfather died, while Chris was with him at the house on McGregor Bay.

It was late summer, and Chris was living in Denver. Cathy had asked him if he would be willing to spend a few weeks in Canada, helping his grandfather, and he readily agreed.

He spent three weeks there, he told me, helping to cook meals and taking his grandfather out on the water for as long as he could manage it.

"We'd just go trawling for bass or pike," Chris recalled. "He'd catch a couple of fish, and it was like he had filled up his cup, and he'd say, 'Okay, I'm done, let's go home.'"

But the summer was coming to its end, and everyone understood it would soon be time to close the house for the season.

One night, Smale made a request of his grandson. He wanted to take one more trip around the bay.

Chris rigged up an armchair in the front of a flat-bottomed boat, and with the trolling motor pushing them along at a snail's pace, they made the circuit of the bay, past familiar points and coves and favorite fishing spots.

"It was his farewell," Chris told me. "We didn't really talk; he just kind of soaked it all in. He knew. He knew he wasn't coming back."

That's how I choose to think about John Smale in his final days, sitting straight-backed, facing forward, moving through the waters that he loved, with the responsibility for guiding the boat passed safely to his grandson. And doing so in silence. Because, between them, there was nothing left to say.

Vision, Humility and Trust: The Lasting Impact of John Smale

David Taylor

Former Executive Chairman of the Board

The Procter & Gamble Company

The first time I heard John Smale speak was in 1989. He had just previously announced that he would be stepping down as CEO, to be succeeded by Ed Artzt, his chosen successor, with the unanimous support of P&G's Board of Directors. At that point, John had been President or Chairman of Procter & Gamble for 16 years and Chief Executive for nine years, capping a 38-year career with P&G.

I had recently been given responsibility as Plant Manager of the Company's paper manufacturing facility in Mehoopany, Pennsylvania, and had been invited to attend the "Year-End Meeting," an annual ritual which brought together several thousand P&G employees. Together, we all sat inside Riverfront Coliseum, a venue normally reserved for rock concerts and other mega-events. For several hours, we listened as P&G leaders from around the world shared the Company's successes, drew lessons from its mistakes, and reinforced the culture of a company that cared deeply about passing along shared wisdom from one generation of leaders to another.

John's comments that day were brief, but I remember his honesty and humility. "There have been many times during these past nine years," he said, "when, in the dark hours of night, I've yearned for more insight, for better answers than I felt I had to problems the business faced. But never — never once did I doubt that I did indeed have your best wishes — and your prayers."

Some time later, John Pepper — a mentor to me — gave me a copy of the remarks John Smale had delivered nine years before when he first became CEO. P&G had just come through an extremely challenging decade and was headed into an uncertain new one. John told the organization that he wanted to share his "sense of the future" which, he said, was best described as "optimism and confidence — optimism that this great Company can have an even greater future and confidence that it will."

He talked about P&G's heritage as a future-focused strength. He described opportunities for growth that included the globalization of our business. He reinforced the central importance of innovation and the power of iconic brands. And he provided a clear-eyed assessment of how difficult it would be to meet the decade's mounting challenges. But through it all, he kept coming back to his optimism and confidence and the level of performance that he felt P&G people should be expecting of themselves — himself included.

I didn't know it then, but the substance and tone of those two talks to the organization — his first and his last as CEO — would help shape my leadership style and those of so many others. He role-modeled what it takes to create the future by placing confidence and trust in those who would build it, with his characteristic blend of humility and vision. In doing so, he influenced generations of leaders through whom he continues to have a meaningful impact on business today.

Over the course of my career at P&G, I had many more opportunities to learn from John. Much of what I learned I drew from his speeches, which John Pepper continually shared with me. We'd discuss the wisdom in those remarks and how to apply them to the leadership challenges I was facing at any given point in my career. Three lessons, in particular, stand out most prominently for me as I reflect on them today.

First, leadership comes from personal presence and actions, not positional power. This is as true for the leader of a small team as it is for the leader of a global institution. John was a towering role model who didn't fit the stereotype of a towering role model. He wasn't charismatic. He was serious, soft-spoken, and sometimes stern. But he had a presence that built confidence in people and motivated them without the need for theatrics or exhortation. It came from his vision, his courage, his belief in others, and his integrity. He role-modeled what I think of as "quiet leadership" — the kind of leadership that gets through the noise of the present and makes a difference that lasts.

Second, innovation is the only sustainable source of growth and vitality. John never wavered in his commitment to industry-leading and often game-changing innovation. He was a tireless champion of innovators and deeply respected their scientific, technical and creative expertise. He was also a tireless enemy of bureaucracy and any other barrier that got in the way of great innovation. Internal processes and systems were never an excuse for under-performance in John's eyes; he fought throughout his career to replace bureaucracy with a spirit of entrepreneurialism — and he unleashed the power of innovators in every part of the business as a result.

Third, an organization's strength is driven by the depth and diversity of its talent. Just as he invested in innovation, John invested relentlessly in people. He did so organizationally, through his commitment to global diversity, rewards systems, and organizational structures that enabled people to flourish. But, he also invested in people on a personal level as I learned from the stories and lessons shared with me by John Pepper and many others who were around him. John Smale was remarkably generous with his time and insights, helping people see what he saw and reach potential that they may not even have seen in themselves — and, most importantly, providing people with opportunities to reach beyond their grasp. If John asked you to step up to a responsibility, it was virtually impossible to say no. You knew he wouldn't have asked if he didn't believe you had the capability to do what he was asking, no matter how daunting the challenge. John taught so many that there is no more powerful form of leadership than high standards and deep trust.

There's much more to draw from the "John Smale Well" than these three lessons, but as I read this book and reflected on all that I've learned from John and those that he directly taught and mentored who I worked more closely with — these are the three that feel most relevant today and that I am confident will continue to stand the test of time.

There is no doubt in my mind that the companies John led — Procter & Gamble and General Motors — would not be the companies they are today without his leadership. His presence is very much alive in these companies, even for people who never knew him or perhaps have never even heard his name. His influence isn't always visible, but it is indelible.

More importantly, though, is that John's leadership transcends these two iconic companies. He is a role model for every leader in every organization at every level. He made all of us feel that we were part of something special, something bigger than ourselves. He inspired the best in us by expecting the most of us. And he never asked any of us for anything that he did not require of himself.

This is why John Smale still matters. And always will.

David Taylor

John G. Smale Chronology

1927   Born in Listowel, Ontario, Canada

1949   Graduated from Miami University
        Joined Vick Chemical Company

1950   Married Phyllis Weaver

1952   Joined Procter & Gamble as Assistant Brand Manager

1954   Brand Manager

1958   Associate Advertising Manager

1963   Manager, Advertising Department, Toilet Goods Division

1966   Manager, Toilet Goods Division

1967   Vice President, Toilet Goods Division

1968   Vice President, Bar Soap and Household Cleaning Products Division

1969   Vice President, Packaged Soap and Detergent Division

1970   Vice President - Group Executive

1972   Member, P&G Board of Directors

1973   Executive Vice President

1974   President

1981   President and Chief Executive Officer

1986   Chairman of the Board and Chief Executive Officer, P&G

1990   Retired as Chairman of the Board and Chief Executive Officer, P&G

Chairman of the Executive Committee of the Board of Directors,

P&G

1992   Chairman of the Board of Directors, General Motors

1995   Retired from P&G Board of Directors

1996   Chairman of the Executive Committee of the Board of Directors,

General Motors

2000   Retired from GM Board of Directors

2011   Died at his home in Cincinnati, Ohio

Acknowledgements

Above all, I want to thank my wife, Stacey Dash. Without her love, encouragement, and support, this book — and so, so much else — would have been impossible. I love her more with every passing day.

I also want to thank our three children, Ryan and Andrew Garver and Lauren Thiell, for their love and patience when, "He's working on the book" was, for so long, the explanation for why I was holed up in my office.

My mother, Elizabeth Garver, was an indispensable touchstone for the parts of this book that are about my father's life, and an insightful editor of the remainder. My siblings and siblings-in-law were, likewise, enormously helpful in both ways they surely know, and others they may not. Thanks, Tom and Jenn Garver, Jen and John Landis, and Karin Garver.

If this book has a heart, it is Cathy Caldemeyer. She inspired me with her conviction that her father was a man whose memory ought not to be allowed to fade away. Cathy's patience and her willingness to take the "long view" as the project unfolded were themselves a fitting tribute to John Smale.

If this book has a soul, it is John Pepper, whose tireless work to make it a reality and passionate advocacy for its importance gave me the confidence to keep moving forward. John's belief in the importance of the stories told in this book animated this project from beginning to end.

This book would not have been completed without the unwavering support of Greg Icenhower. Greg's understanding of what this book could be was, at several points in its creation, far clearer than my own. Without his vision, wise counsel and sharp editorial eye, *Here Forever* would not exist.

Chris Caldemeyer's insights into his grandfather's character were an indispensable element of this book. I am also deeply grateful to Smale's children, grandchildren, and other relatives for their time and support. Thank you, Jay and Joanne Smale, Lisa Durham, Rob Caldemeyer, Lisa Diedrichs, Madeline Caldemeyer, Emma Durham and Sam Durham. Special thanks go to Peter Smale who, in addition to sitting for lengthy interviews, collected and processed the photos that illustrate this book.

Ed Artzt, John Smale's close friend and successor as chairman and CEO of Procter & Gamble, welcomed me into his home, sat for hours of interviews, and patiently read draft after draft of this book. Ed's insights and memories are woven into every chapter of *Here Forever*.

Gordon Brunner, the former chief technology officer of P&G, was one of the first people I interviewed when I began my research. He helped me see the rich trove of stories about Smale's commitment to innovation that was available to me. His dedication to seeing Smale's story told was an inspiration.

I am very appreciative of Paul Fox, Ed Tazzia, and the entire P&G alumni network for the outpouring of stories and recollections about Smale that added so much color to the book.

Shane Meeker, P&G's company historian and corporate storyteller; Greg McCoy, P&G's senior archivist; and Lori Cornwell, P&G's processing archivist, provided a trove of data and documents about Smale that were crucial building blocks of the book.

Jim Stengel, a former global marketing officer at P&G, provided key insights and valuable counsel in the early stages of this book's creation.

Marc Pritchard, P&G's chief brand officer, was an early and enthusiastic supporter of this project, and contributed greatly to its success.

Damon Jones, P&G's chief communications officer, was a valuable sounding board for the team during this book's development.

My thanks go out to Pete Blackshaw and the Cintrifuse team who, at crucial moments in this book's development, generously provided working space in Cincinnati's unique and vibrant Union Hall.

I am deeply grateful to Evelyn Duffy, Scott Butterworth, and Anna Fiorino, of Open Boat Editing, whose work on the manuscript of this book brought focus and clarity to the storytelling.

Natalie Hastings, of Limelight PR, brought invaluable expertise to the effort to put *Here Forever* in front of as many readers as we possibly could.

Doug Conant, of ConantLeadership, and former CEO of Campbell Soup Company, was a wonderful advocate for the story of John Smale, and a huge force in helping raise awareness about the timelessness of the book's lessons.

Working under tight time constraints, and despite late changes to the text, Cathy Seckman did a superb job in assembling the index of *Here Forever*.

Sue Hermanns provided important organizational support including identifying and tracking down many of the people I interviewed in my research into John Smale's life.

Andrew and Jennifer Niemann, and Sarah Swanson helped me immensely by providing a copy of David Swanson's personal memoir.

Dozens of current and former Procter & Gamble employees gave generously of their time and attention to make sure that the story of John Smale was fully told. They include Susan Arnold, Chip Bergh, Wolfgang Berndt, Barb Buerkle, Bob Blanchard, Jerry Dirvin, Jason Duff, Kathy Fish, George Gibson, Bob Gill, Bob Haxby, Helen Hoffman, Jane Hoover, Durk Jager, Ceil Kuzma, Tom Laco, A.G. Lafley, Bob McDonald, Bob Merold, Tamara Minick-Scokalo, Jorge Montoya, Tom Muccio, Charlotte Otto, Paul Polman, Lou Pritchett, Janet Reid, Ann Schulte, Susan Tiemeier Franz, Paul Trokhan, Dave Walker, Bob Wehling, Peg Wyant, Mick Yates, and Wahib Zaki.

Among the people who helped me tell the story of John Smale's time at General Motors were Craig Buchholz, Ira Millstein, Harry Pearce, Sally Sasso, Jack Smith, Maria Van Neumann Whitman, and Rick Wagoner.

Other friends and associates of John Smale who gave me their time to help round out the story of his life include Norm Augustine, Geoff Boisi, Bill Burleigh, Frank Caccamo, Paul Fitzgerald, Bert Hulgrave, Rich Kiley, Marje Kiley, Charlie Luken, Charlie Mechem, James O'Reilly and John Ruthven.

Others who provided valuable support and encouragement include Roy Bostock, the former chairman and CEO of D'Arcy Masius Benton & Bowles; Jenny Darroch, dean of the Farmer School of Business at Miami University; Zach First, the director of the Drucker Institute; and Bob Iger, the former chairman and CEO of the Walt Disney Company.

Special thanks to Frank McElwain, the artist who painted the cover portrait of John Smale, and to Procter & Gamble and General Motors, for making archival photos of Smale and his colleagues available.

Index

Page numbers in italics indicate photos, illustrations

G